1000 Doctor Who Facts

Scott Ambrose

CONTENTS

INTRODUCTION

Doctor Who is a beloved and iconic British science fiction television series that has captured the hearts of audiences around the world for over five decades. From its humble beginnings in 1963 to its current incarnation as a global phenomenon, the show has enchanted viewers with its imaginative storytelling, intriguing characters, and groundbreaking special effects.

Join us on a journey through time and space as we explore the fascinating world of Doctor Who and delve into the countless facts, trivia, and behind-the-scenes secrets that have made it a cultural institution. Whether you're a seasoned Whovian or a curious newcomer, this fact book is sure to delight and entertain as we uncover the mysteries of the Time Lord and his incredible adventures throughout the universe.

1000 DOCTOR WHO FACTS

(1) The Stones of Blood clearly owes something to Children of the Stones. Children of the Stones is a 1976 British children's drama created by Jeremy Burnham and Trevor Ray. It ran for seven episodes (which when all put together now make it like a long feature length film) and is regarded to be something of a cult series. The story has a scientist and his teenage son moving to a village named Milbury which is ringed by megalithic stones. It doesn't take too long for them to notice that there is something rather strange about the occupants of the village.

(2) Remembrance of the Daleks: Part One features a slice of Doctor Who history because we see a Dalek navigate some stairs - something which the Fourth Doctor mocked them for not being able to do. It had been implied before though that the Daleks could levitate.

(3) The pop star Rachel Stevens, of S Club 7 fame, was one of the final two contenders for the part of Rose Tyler but lost out to Billie Piper.

(4) The two part finale to 2024's 'season one' had more than its fair share of things for fans to nitpick. One of the most obvious complaints was that Sutekh was back and yet the Fourteenth Doctor, living down the road with his own TARDIS, was nowhere to be seen! Surely someone would have given him a quick call wouldn't they?

(5) Orphan 55 has some allusions to The Time Machine - where in the 83rd Century humanity has devolved into two separate races. The beautiful, childlike and thoughtless Eloi live out an idle, vacuous existence on the surface while the

subterranean troglodytic Morlocks lurk underground and prey on the Eloi when night falls.

(6) The River Song arc in Doctor Who is patently inspired by The Time Traveler's Wife. The Time Traveler's Wife is a novel written by Audrey Niffenegger that follows the complex relationship between Henry DeTamble, a man with a genetic disorder that causes him to involuntarily time travel, and his wife Clare Abshire. The story unfolds in a non-linear fashion, shifting between Henry and Clare's perspectives as they navigate the challenges of their unconventional love story. Steven Moffat later adapted The Time Traveler's Wife
for television - though it didn't get very good reviews or last for very long.

(7) Susan Foreman is the Doctor's granddaughter and featured in the early years of the show. Anthony Coburn, a writer on the show when it began, came up with the idea of making Susan a relative of the Doctor because he felt the optics of William Hartnell's mature Doctor knocking around with a teenage girl on his travels was a bit weird.

(8) Tip Tipping was a stunt co-ordinator on Doctor Who in the late 80s. Tipping played Private Crowe in the classic sci-fi sequel Aliens. Tipping had also served in the SAS - a famous special forces unit of the British Army. He sadly died in a 1993 parachuting accident.

(9) If you count both of the Russell T Davies eras of showrunning Doctor Who, his lowest rated episode on IMDB is 2024's Space Babies - which, at the time of writing, stands at a dismal 5.2 out of 10.

(10) The Doctor Who episode Planet Of Evil owes quite a lot to the classic 1956 film Forbidden Planet. Forbidden Planet was

directed by Fred M. Wilcox. The script was by Cyril Hume and based on an original film story by Allen Adler and Irving Block. Shakespeare's The Tempest was patently an influence on the story. The film is set in the 23rd century and follows a crew from Earth who arrive on the distant planet Altair-IV to investigate the fate of a previous expedition. They discover the lone survivors, the brilliant but enigmatic Dr Morbius (Walter Pidgeon), and his daughter Altaira (Anne Francis), who reside in a high-tech paradise created by an ancient alien race called the Krell. As the crew explores the planet, they encounter strange phenomena and a powerful invisible creature that threatens their safety.

(11) It was Tom Baker's idea for his Doctor to be partial to jelly babies. Jelly babies are soft jelly sugar sweets. They were first made in Lancashire in 1864.

(12) Nine of the ten lowest rated episodes of NuWho on IMDB are all from the Chris Chibnall era.

(13) 1972's The Three Doctors was the first 'multi Doctor' special. It featured Jon Pertwee, Patrick Troughton, and William Hartnell.

(14) During the Tom Baker era you could actually buy licenced Doctor Who baked beans in the supermarket.

(15) The Thirteenth Doctor's crystal TARDIS interior was by all accounts a nightmare to shoot in because it was too cramped.

(16) The plot of the second half of the episode 73 Yards patently owes a lot to the Stephen King book The Dead Zone - which was turned into a pretty good 1983 film.

(17) Philip Hinchcliffe was the showrunner from 1974-77. Many feel this was the most consistent Doctor Who era. Among the episodes Hinchcliffe oversaw were The Ark In Space, Genesis Of The Daleks, Terror Of The Zygons, and The Pyramids Of Mars.

(18) Apart from the cricket jumper, Peter Davison said said he didn't like his Edwardian themed costume very much.

(19) The first licenced Doctor Who video game was 1983's Doctor Who: The First Adventure for the BBC Micro. This game (which unavoidably looks primitive by today's standards) was composed of four minigames which were clearly inspired by arcade classics like Frogger and Space Invaders.

(20) There was something different about Rose Tyler when she came back in 2008. She looked different and her voice sounded strange. The explanation for this is that Billie Piper had just had dental surgery to get rid of her overbite. She just didn't quite seem like Rose Tyler anymore without the old teeth and overbite and the recent surgery seemed to have affected her voice.

(21) K-9 and Company was a 1981 pilot for a spin-off show. It featured Elisabeth Sladen as Sarah Jane Smith and John Leeson as the voice of K·9. Though it got pretty good viewing figures it was not commissioned as a series because of a change at the top of BBC One.

(22) The 2024 series of Doctor Who is slightly confusing in that Russell T Davies billed it as season one and yet it was usually dubbed season fourteen in the media and press.

(23) John Simm returning as the Master in season ten was

completely ruined by a BBC trailer for the forthcoming episodes.

(24) Nicola Bryant got frostbite and pneumonia while filming The Caves of Androzani: Part One because it was freezing but she had to wear Peri's summer outfit.

(25) Andrew Cartmel, a script editor on Classic Who, was critical of Chris Chibnall's Timeless Child arc because he felt it 'depleted' the mystery of the Doctor.

(26) Jon Pertwee served with future James Bond author Ian Fleming in an intelligence division during the war.

(27) The little girl who plays Squeak in the Seventh Doctor story Survival is Adele Silva. Adele Silva would later become a familiar face on British television through her role as Kelly Windsor in the soap opera Emmerdale.

(28) The huge skyscraper tower that UNIT operate from in latter NuWho clearly takes a lot of inspiration from the Avengers tower in the Marvel films.

(29) The Daleks, sinister aliens in metal pepperpot transporters forever bent on universal conquest, were a wondrous Terry Nation creation and terrified generations of children.

(30) Voyage of the Damned was plainly inspired by The Poseidon Adventure. The Poseidon Adventure is a disaster film based on the novel of the same name by Paul Gallico. Directed by Ronald Neame, the film was released in 1972 and follows the story of a luxury ocean liner, the SS Poseidon, that capsizes after being hit by a massive tidal wave.

(31) The highest rated episode of NuWho on IMDB is Blink with a score of 9.8 out of ten.

(32) Michael Grade was the man who axed Doctor Who in the 1980s and sent it into limbo. Grade was the controller of BBC One at the time. Michael Grade was no fan of science fiction and seemed to have a particular disdain for Doctor Who - which he thought was cheap and rubbish.

(33) A very young Chris Chibnall appeared on BBC feedback show Open Air in 1986 representing the Doctor Who Appreciation Society. He was critical of the Doctor Who writers Pip and Jane Baker and clearly unimpressed by the show. This appearance on Open Air was obviously a bit embarrassing for Chris when he became a writer and then showrunner on Doctor Who many years later.

(34) The lowest rated episode on IMDB from the first Russell T Davies era as showrunner is Fear Her - which scored just 5.8 out of ten.

(35) 1965's Dr Who and the Daleks was the first of two films Amicus Productions made based on the BBC television show. Amicus bought an option from the BBC to make two Doctor Who films for the modest sum of £500. Amicus (Latin for "friendship") Productions were created by Americans Milton Subotsky and Max J Rosenberg and - inspired by Hammer's fame - they gate-crashed the thriving (if thrifty) British horror scene. Rosenberg was a lawyer by trade while Subotsky was a horror and sci-fi buff who had worked as an editor in the army.

At the time the British Government had an incentive that forced cinemas to show a quota of British made films and also offered tax breaks to British based productions. There was money to be made if you were shrewd enough and the Amicus horror legacy became a memorably enjoyable and colourful one.

(36) Amicus released Dr Who and the Daleks under the newly created AARU production banner in order to separate this family film from their usual (and soon to be far more frequent) horror fare. Another salient reason for this is that the financier Joe Vegoda owned AARU and had been instrumental in helping to fund the production budget of Dr Who and the Daleks. In return for putting his hands in his pockets, Vegoda wanted his company to get some promotion through the film. As far as the actual production went though this was still very much an Amicus film.

(37) The main motivation of Amicus for buying the rights to Doctor Who films was the 'Dalekmania' sweeping Britain at the time. People just couldn't get enough of the Daleks. The decision by Amicus to make these films was a shrewd one as they were very popular in the domestic (British) box-office market and children in particular loved them. As for adults and Doctor Who fans, well, they tend to be a lot more lukewarm about the Amicus films based on Doctor Who. The films are aimed squarely at a young audience.

(38) Alex Kingston was the only person who was told what the true identity of River Song was going to be. David Tennant and Matt Smith said that not knowing who River Song really was helped their performances.

(39) Richard Hurndall sadly died only five months after The Five Doctors (in which he played the First Doctor) came out.

(40) Douglas Adams, who was a script editor on Doctor Who for a time, said that Tom Baker constantly oscillated between

being the most charming man in the world to someone you'd happily throw off a cliff.

(41) Doctor Who was revived in 2005 by writer and producer Russell T Davies. Everything after 2005 tends to be known as NuWho in fandom. What came previously is generally designated as Classic Who.

(42) The famous comic book author Grant Morrison expressed a desire to write for the Doctor Who television show and even had a season long arc planned out. However, nothing came of this. Steven Moffat was the showrunner at the time.

(43) Jon Pertwee and Tom Baker had something in common in that they were both in Amicus horror anthology films. Jon was in The House That Dripped Blood while Tom was in Vault of Horror.

(44) Roger Delgado will forever be enshrined in Doctor Who history as the first actor to play the Master - a role he was born to play. Delgado's life ended tragically in 1973 when a car he was driven in while working in Turkey veered off a road and crashed into a ravine.

(45) Steven Moffat said he got the idea for a spaceship having two different timezones in World Enough and Time from his young son.

(46) Peter Jeffrey was on the shortlist to play the Second Doctor but wasn't interested. He later played Count Grendel in The Androids of Tara. Horror fans will probably remember Peter Jeffrey as Inspector Trout in the two Dr Phibes films with Vincent Price.

(47) Revenge of the Cybermen was the first Doctor Who story

to get a release on home video in Britain. This happened in 1983.

(48) Nestlé released a couple of lines of Doctor Who branded chocolate in the 1970s.

(49) The comedy duo Hale & Pace appeared as shop-keepers Harvey and Len in Part One of the 1989 Doctor Who story Survival. Gareth Hale and Norman Pace had a fairly successful sketch show on television and were very famous in the late eighties and early 90s.

(50) David Tennant obviously did not use his own Scottish accent when he played the Doctor. Russell T Davies said that after Christopher Eccleston's northern accented Doctor he didn't want to do a 'tour of the regions' when it came to the Doctor's accent.

(51) Patrick Troughton's Doctor copped some criticism at first because people were so used to Bill Hartnell and had never had to adjust to a new Doctor before. They soon warmed to the Second Doctor though and thanks to Troughton the viewers got used to the fact that Doctor Who would change its lead actor from time to time.

(52) Sir Ridley Scott briefly worked on a designer on Doctor Who in the 1960s.

(53) Matt Smith didn't watch Doctor Who growing up because it had been axed and wasn't on telly.

(54) Terry Nation said he created the Daleks to avoid the 'man in rubber suit' monster trope of low-budget science fiction.

(55) The Amicus film Dr Who and the Daleks is not considered

to be part of the Doctor Who canon or history but just its own thing completely separate from the BBC's version of Doctor Who on television. In this film, the Doctor is not an alien Time Lord from the planet Gallifrey but an eccentric human inventor. At the time this was actually in line with the television show because all the lore about Gallifrey and Time Lords had yet to be established.

(56) William Hartnell was not asked to reprise his television role as the Doctor for the Amicus film Dr Who and the Daleks (which apparently annoyed Hartnell because he would have loved to do a Doctor Who film) and so the Doctor was instead played by Amicus favourite Peter Cushing. It appears that Amicus decided that William Hartnell wasn't well known outside of Britain and wanted a more famous actor to play the Doctor.

(57) Peter Cushing, in a performance that was not to all tastes, deploys his rather comic 'doddery old man' routine for the part of the Doctor in Dr Who and the Daleks. Peter Cushing's version of the Doctor is a bumbling sweet grandfather who is smart but sort of clumsy.

(58) Terry Nation later expressed what you might call a lack of enthusiasm for Peter Cushing's Doctor in the Amicus films. "He was a little too gentle... too kindly and too warm. The thing that Bill (Hartnell) had was this irascibility... he was a bad tempered, old, curmudgeonly figure... I'd like to have seen more of that in the character."

(59) Jodie Whittaker said that when she was offered a Doctor Who audition by Chris Chibnall she was given two weeks to decide if she wanted to do the test but in the end only needed 24 hours to say yes.

(60) Carole Ann Ford left her role as the Doctor's granddaughter Susan in 1964 because she felt there wasn't an awful lot for her character to do. She did though play Susan again in The Five Doctors.

(61) The Five Doctors is a special feature-length episode which originally aired in 1983 to celebrate the show's 20th anniversary. The episode features Patrick Troughton, Jon Pertwee, and Peter Davison. Richard Hurndall played the First Doctor because William Hartnell had passed away. Tom Baker declined to participate and is represented through archive footage.

(62) Tom Baker declined to take part in The Five Doctors because he'd only recently left the show. He also said he had no interest in an episode where he would only be playing 20% of the Doctor's role.

(63) You could buy Doctor Who sweet cigarettes in 1964. Sweet cigarettes were an edible candy shaped like cigarettes and sold to kids.

(64) The Thirteenth Doctor has a custard cream dispenser in her TARDIS. Jodie Whittaker was not told about this so her delighted surprise in the scene is genuine.

(65) It was Peter Capaldi's idea for his Doctor to play the guitar and wear sonic sunglasses. Some fans found the guitar and sunglasses a bit naff.

(66) Tom Baker tended to only learn his own lines and not read the other parts of the scripts. He did this so the Doctor's reactions to other characters would feel more genuine.

(67) Terry Nation said he went to the United States in the mid

1960s and unsuccessfully tried to sell the idea of a show about the Daleks to networks over there. The Doctor couldn't have been in the show because the BBC owned that but Nation had the Dalek rights.

(68) Tom Baker said he didn't like the two Doctor Who films with Peter Cushing. He thought they were a bit too silly and lightweight.

(69) The dinosaur special effects in Invasion of the Dinosaurs have not aged very well at all. Barry Letts admitted the dinosaurs were pretty terrible. They'd just use CGI today but back in 1974 they obviously didn't have that option.

(70) Mary Whitehouse, who was the founder of the National Viewers' and Listeners' Association, and a sort of self-appointed moral guardian, made several complaints against Doctor Who. She took particular offence at the Doctor seeming to drown in The Deadly Assassin.

(71) Scream of the Shalka is an animated Doctor Who story that was released in 2003 as part of the show's 40th-anniversary celebrations. The story follows the Doctor, played by Richard E. Grant, as he arrives in the small English village of Lannet and must save the villagers from a deadly alien invasion led by the monstrous Shalka.

(72) Class was a 2016 Doctor Who spin-off show set at Coal Hill Academy. Peter Capaldi made an appearance as the Doctor in one episode and it was executive produced by Steven Moffat. The show aired on BBC3 and only lasted eight episodes until it was axed. Although the show got fairly decent (if middling) reviews it never found an audience or quite seemed to work out what audience it was actually going for.

(73) Faye Marsay appeared in the 2014 Doctor Who Christmas special Last Christmas as Shona. Her character in the episode mentions planning a Game of Thrones marathon. A year later Faye Marsay was actually in Game of Thrones. She played the Waif - the character who torments Arya in Braavos

(74) Robert Holmes was famous for doing extensive rewrites of the Doctor Who scripts. This irritated a lot of the writers because no writer likes to see their work altered - even if it might be for the better.

(75) Many fans of Classic Who have said that if Robert Holmes was the script editor in the modern era then Chris Chibnall and Russell T Davies would have been lucky to have 10% of their scripts survive into the finished draft! One can't imagine Holmes would be too impressed by things like Orphan 55 and Space Babies.

(76) Paul McGann actually had a shaved head when he did the Doctor Who television movie because he came off another part where he played a soldier. His hair as the Doctor was a luxurious wig.

(77) Matt Smith is the youngest actor to play the Doctor. He was only 26 when he auditioned for the part.

(78) John Nathan Turner was the showrunner (producer) who doggedly kept Doctor Who going in the 1980s until it was finally put out to pasture by Michael Grade. John Nathan Turner is an infamous figure in Doctor Who history because of the inconsistent nature of his era and his fondness for gimmicky stunt casting. His passion for Doctor Who was never in doubt though. Some retrospectives of John Nathan-Turner have alleged he used his position of authority to sleep with as many teenagers as he could.

(79) Tom Baker and Elisabeth Sladen hated the script for The Android Invasion so much they actually changed some of their lines themselves.

(80) A British police box is a type of public telephone kiosk that was originally used by police officers to communicate with their headquarters while out on patrol. The boxes were usually (though not always) blue and originally designed in 1929. The telephone in the box was connected to the local police headquarters. These boxes were used up until the late 1960s before they were phased out.

(81) The Thirteenth Doctor's biscuit of choice is the custard cream but Matt Smith's Doctor was very fond of Jammie Dodgers.

(82) Colin Baker becomes noticeably beefier during his run as the Doctor. He was gaining weight in real life and later diagnosed with diabetes.

(83) Gallifrey is first mentioned by name in The Time Warrior.

(84) The Seeds Of Doom is patently inspired by The Thing From Another World. The Thing from Another World is a 1951 science fiction/horror film. Although Christian Nyby is officially listed as the director it is sometimes alleged that the film was in fact directed by Howard Hawks. Nyby worked as an editor on several Howard Hawks films. The film was based on the 1938 novella Who Goes There? by John W Campbell and is one of the more influential results of the classic fifties monster/paranoia sci-fi boom.

(85) Terry Nation said the Daleks were partly inspired by the Nazis but they also represent a sort of faceless 'officialdom'. They are a blank and terrifying authority.

(86) Tosin Cole got heatstroke while filming The Ghost Monument in South Africa.

(87) Terry Nation sat in on a few production meetings for the Amicus film Dr Who and the Daleks but evidently didn't want to write the film himself.

(88) The 1965 film Dr Who and the Daleks was directed by Gordon Flemyng and written by Milton Subotsky. It is said though that David Whitaker really wrote the film on the instruction of Terry Nation - Nation allowing Subotsky to have the screen credit as along as Whitaker was brought in as a writer.

(89) A young Martin Clunes appeared in the Doctor Who story Snakedance. Clunes has since made light of the preposterous costumes he had to wear in Who.

(90) Rodney Bewes was a guest star in Resurrection of the Daleks. Bewes was best known for his role as Bob Ferris in The Likely Lads and Whatever Happened to the Likely Lads? The television career of Bewes was fading fast at this point and he later said that Doctor Who royalties were very welcome.

(91) Geoffrey Bayldon was approached to be the First Doctor but declined because he considered himself too young for the part and he also wasn't too keen on the proposed shooting schedule. Bayldon would appear in many things in his long career. Amicus horror films, Catweazle, and also as the Crowman alongside Jon Pertwee in Worzel Gummidge.

(92) Richard Hurndall said that when he played the First Doctor in The Five Doctors he didn't try to impersonate William Hartnell. What he did was try to bring some of of Hartnell's mannerisms to his performance rather than mimic

Hartnell.

(93) Peter Davison said that the cheap TARDIS interior in Classic Who was not helped by always being shot in bright light. He thought it would have looked much better with dimmer or more atmospheric lighting.

(94) Jon Pertwee was something of an action man in real life too. He loved scuba diving and rode his motorbike into his seventies.

(95) In the early days of Doctor Who they tended to just do one take of a scene. You can see William Hartnell flub a few lines of dialogue here and there but - like an old pro - just carry on and make the best of it.

(96) Spearhead From Space was the first serial to be made in colour.

(97) Peter Cushing said he turned down an offer to play the Doctor in the BBC television series twice in the 1960s because he wanted to make films rather than work on the small screen.

(98) 1980s showrunner John Nathan Turner disliked the sonic screwdriver because he felt it was a cheap gimmick which made it too easy for the Doctor to get out of difficult situations.

(99) Janet Fielding said she was always frozen doing outdoor location work because the clothes Tegan wore were not really suitable for cold weather.

(100) Patrick Wymark turned down an approach to become the Second Doctor. Wymark was in films like When Eagles

Dare and Witchfinder General. He sadly died in 1970 at the age of 44.

(101) When the show returned in 2005 after its long hiatus, references to Classic Who were minimal in the first season because Russell T Davies didn't want to confuse new younger viewers who were unfamiliar with the show.

(102) The title Arachnids in the UK is a (weak) pun on the Sex Pistols song Anarchy in the UK.

(103) In the film Dr Who and the Daleks, an accident propels the Doctor, his granddaughters Susan (Roberta Tovey), Barbara (Jennie Linden), and Barbara's boyfriend Ian (Roy Castle), through time and space in the TARDIS to a dying planet where a city is occupied by those metal encased intergalactic villains the Daleks. The Daleks are intent on wiping out a race of humans known as the Thals and - needless to say - the Doctor and his friends become embroiled in all the drama and danger.

(104) The regeneration of Colin Baker into Sylvester McCoy in Time and the Rani is famously terrible because Colin declined to take part (you couldn't really blame him for not turning up given that he'd been fired by the BBC). As a consequence of this Sylvester had to don a curly wig and pretend to be Colin!

(105) There was a K-9 spin-off show in 2009 which was an Australian co-production. References to Doctor Who in the show were absent due to rights issues. The show got pretty terrible reviews.

(106) John Nathan Turner said scripts being stolen and leaked before the episodes went out was a problem during his era on the show. He even saw a leaked script for sale at a convention

once!

(107) The lowest rated episode from Steven Moffat's era as showrunner on IMDB is Sleep No More - which scored 5.8 out of ten.

(108) Janet Fielding said she really loathed the white outfit Tegan wore in Arc of Infinity.

(109) Billie Piper was born Leian Piper.

(110) Elisabeth Sladen created continuity havoc during her time on the show by cutting her hair before Invasion of the Dinosaurs.

(111) Lord of the Rings director Peter Jackson, who is a big Doctor Who fan, was supposed to direct an episode in the Peter Capaldi era but sadly this never happened in the end.

(112) Amy and Rory were the first married couple to travel with the Doctor.

(113) The Kandyman in The Happiness Patrol is patently made of giant Liquorice Allsorts. Bassett's, who made this confectionery, complained about the similarity between the Kandyman and Bertie Bassett - their Liquorice Allsorts mascot. As a consequence, the BBC had to promise not to use the Kandyman again.

(114) The Third Doctor was known for his dapper appearance, fondness for gadgets, and his love of fancy cars, particularly his trusty yellow roadster known as Bessie.

(115) Matt Smith was a talented footballer as a youngster. He was in the Nottingham Forest youth squad.

(116) Terry Nation, post Doctor Who, created the cultish sci-fi shows Blake's 7 and Survivors.

(117) The Daleks armed with what seem to be fire extinguishers in the film Dr Who and the Daleks was done because Amicus wanted a U certificate for the film. They feared that if the Daleks were slaughtering people left, right, and centre with death rays then they might not have the family film they set out to make.

(118) The Zygons are shape-shifting aliens from the planet Zygor who are capable of taking on the appearance of any other living being

(119) Christopher Eccleston said that on his first block of filming on Doctor Who, the relationship between him and the 'showrunner, the producer, and co-producer – broke down irreparably and it never recovered.'

(120) Michael Grade, while admitting that Doctor Who is never going to be his cup of tea, was at least gracious enough to say he was impressed by the production values of the 2005 reboot of Doctor Who.

(121) Patrick Troughton said he tried to make his Doctor a listener. Someone who takes in all points of view and then comes to a decision.

(122) A spin-off show titled Rose Tyler: Earth Defence was floated before the departure of Billie Piper but never went into production. It is believed that one of the reasons why the show never happened is that Billie Piper wanted to do something new and wasn't keen on playing Rose again.

(123) Doctor Who: Dimensions in Time is a special crossover

episode that aired in 1993 as part of the Children in Need telethon. The episode sees several incarnations of the Doctor teaming up to battle the villainous Rani and the Master as they attempt to disrupt the time continuum. The special was met with mixed reviews from fans and critics, with some comparing it to the much derided Star Wars Holiday Special.

(124) The British Rocket Group is mentioned in Remembrance of the Daleks. This is obviously a Quartermass reference.

(125) Jon Pertwee's Doctor was mostly confined to Earth to keep the budget under control.

(126) Matthew Waterhouse was a big Doctor Who fan so joining the show as Adric was a dream to him. However, he said the experience was not always pleasant. Tom Baker was quite aloof towards him at times and there was an uneasy atmosphere on the set because Baker and Lalla Ward (who were married in real life) were not getting on very well and argued a lot.

(127) One of the best directors of the NuWho era is Rachel Talalay. She directed classic episodes like Heaven Sent and The Doctor Falls. Rachel Talalay's first directing credit was the horror sequel Freddy's Dead: The Final Nightmare.

(128) Segun Akinola was the music composer during the Chris Chibnall era. Segun's music was very interesting by dint of being so different from Murray Gold.

(129) Roberta Tovey plays the Doctor's smart scientific minded young granddaughter in the film Dr Who and the Daleks. Apparently the director, in order to speed up the production, offered Tovey a shilling every time she successfully did a take in one go and she became so

accomplished at this she ended up costing him a small fortune!

(130) The Tom Baker era story Robot is patently inspired by (among other things) King Kong.

(131) David Tennant was a big Doctor Who fan as a kid. His favourite Doctor was Peter Davison.

(132) Matthew Waterhouse said his acting career fizzled out after Doctor Who because he was just seen as 'that kid from Doctor Who' and wasn't taken seriously.

(133) When it was announced Doctor Who was coming back in 2005 there was a lot of scepticism over whether it would work in a more modern era or be any good. Happily though the new show confounded expectations and was a success with both critics and viewers.

(134) Jon Pertwee said he quite surprised people by giving a very straight performance as the Doctor because everyone knew him as a comic character actor and were expecting him to play it funny and eccentric. Jon Pertwee was essentially a comic character actor so he enjoyed confounding expectations by playing a very in command and confident Doctor when he took over the role.

(135) Peter Cushing said the following of the two Doctor Who films he made for Amicus - "They were very enjoyable. A little frustrating, though, because they were not quite what we planned. I think I speak for everyone involved when I say that we intended to make them a little darker. But they turned out well, very good entertainments and a hit with the children."

(136) Ncuti Gatwa's Fifteenth Doctor has a habit of calling

people 'honey' and 'babes' - which some fans found a trifle annoying.

(137) Christopher Eccleston was not actually courted for the part of the Doctor when the show came back. It was the other way around. He asked to do an audition when he heard Doctor Who was coming back and that Russell T Davies was writing and producing it.

(138) John Barrowman said that, before he landed the part of Captain Jack, he auditioned for the role of James Bond in 2002.

(139) William Hartnell was in poor health when they made The Three Doctors so the First Doctor only appears on the TARDIS scanner. Hartnell shot his contribution to the special in one day.

(140) Despite his poor health and limited participation, William Hartnell exudes authority in The Three Doctors and makes the most of his lines.

(141) Michelle Ryan played Lady Christina de Souza in Planet of the Dead. Ryan was a familiar face to British audiences through her role as Zoe Slater in EastEnders.

(142) 73 Yards was the first episode filmed for the 2024 series - although it was episode four in the running order. The Doctor is largely absent from the episode because Ncuti Gatwa was still shooting on the Netflix show Sex Education. 73 Yards therefore becomes a nice showcase for Millie Gibson as Ruby.

(143) Colin Baker was nicknamed 'Archie' by some of the writers because his rather arch acting style.

(144) David Tennant filmed his first scene as the Doctor before

the Christopher Eccleston series had even come out. Behind the scenes, Russell T Davies knew that Eccleston wasn't coming back so he moved quickly to get Tennant in place.

(145) The Sea Devils finally returned in Legend of the Sea Devils - the last but one special for the Thirteenth Doctor. Sadly though, the episode turned out to be pretty awful.

(146) The 1996 Doctor Who television movie suggests the Doctor is half-human. This is not considered canon in the television series - although the Eighth Doctor is considered canon.

(147) The Second Doctor was fond of playing the recorder. This was an idea by Patrick Troughton.

(148) John Nathan Turner would get irritated when Sophie Aldred added extra badges to Ace's jacket because it was a nightmare for continuity.

(149) J.K. Rowling was asked if she wanted to write a Doctor Who episode when the show came back in 2005 but she declined the offer because she was too busy.

(150) Some fans were not happy with the way (in their opinion) Steven Moffat's Twice Upon a Time script depicted the First Doctor (played by David Bradley) as some sexist dinosaur.

(151) Doctor Who was originally intended to be an educational show, with episodes focusing on history and science.

(152) Peter Davison was only 29 when he became the Doctor.

(153) Roy Castle is the comic relief in Dr Who and the Daleks

as Ian Chesterton. This is probably another reason why Doctor Who die-hards may not warm to this film. Ian was played in the television show by William Russell as a heroic and forthright sort of character. Roy Castle's version of Ian is closer to Frank Spencer than the Ian of the television show.

(154) Christopher Eccleston later said that he felt Steven Moffat was much better at writing the character of the Doctor than Russell T Davies. However, Eccleston also said that he felt Davies was better at writing for the female companion Rose than Moffat.

(155) Colin Baker said he struggled to get television work after Doctor Who because he had already become typecast in that role - despite his brief tenure.

(156) John Hurt's War Doctor in The Day of The Doctor was supposed to be the Ninth Doctor. The character played by John Hurt was written in as a late replacement because Steven Moffat couldn't persuade Christopher Eccleston to do the special.

(157) Chris Chibnall's series twelve finale the Timeless Children was controversial in fandom because it essentially retconned the backstory of the Doctor. The Timeless Children revealed that the Doctor is not from Gallifrey but began life as small girl from another part of the universe. Then were then endless regenerations before the Doctors we know appeared. William Hartnell has always been the First Doctor. Chris Chibnall retconned the origin of the Doctor so that Hartnell could be the six billionth Doctor now for all we know.

(158) Russell T Davies hasn't said too much about Christopher Eccleston's criticisms of both him and his time on the show. Davies simply said he didn't want to get into a 'tit for tat' with

the actor and praised Christopher Eccleston for being a 'magnificent' Doctor.

(159) Steven Moffat said he asked David Renwick if he'd like to write an episode of Doctor Who but Renwick declined because he didn't like Doctor Who and had no interest in it. David Renwick is best known for writing and creating One Foot in the Grave and Jonathan Creek.

(160) Terry Nation said that when he first heard about Doctor Who he didn't have much confidence that it would work as a show.

(161) Torchwood was a secret codename used by the BBC to disguise copies of yet to be transmitted Doctor Who episodes. Russell T Davies used this name for the spin-off show.

(162) Bonnie Langford got a lot of pelters for her acting performances as Mel in the last embers of 1980s Doctor Who but when she returned many years later she was praised for her acting. Many felt that Bonnie gave the best performance in the 2024 finale Empire of Death.

(163) One grumble fans sometimes have about NuWho is that the companions are always from present day Earth. A number of fans would like an alien companion for a change.

(164) Peter Sallis played Penley in The Ice Warriors. This was several years before Sallis became a familiar face to millions of viewers as Cleggy in Last of the Summer Wine.

(165) Patrick Troughton said the reason he didn't stick with Doctor Who for too long is that he was a character actor and in his opinion it wasn't good for a character actor to become too ingrained in one role. He said he did enjoy his time on

Doctor Who though and loved the character.

(166) City of Death was something of a novelty for Doctor Who because it did location shooting in France. Going abroad was very rare for the meagre budget of Classic Who.

(167) Ken Campbell was considered for the part of the Seventh Doctor. Campbell was a distinctive comic actor who appeared in everything from In Sickness and in Health to Minder. His audition was deemed a bit too dark and eccentric by the BBC.

(168) In a slightly ironic turn of events, the man who beat Ken Campbell to the part of the Seventh Doctor was his protégé Sylvester McCoy. Sylvester McCoy had been recruited by Campbell to the theatrical performance group the Ken Campbell Roadshow. Ken Campbell said, after he was rejected by the BBC, he suggested Sylvester for the part of the Doctor.

(169) The Frontios security forces in the story Frontios wear Federation hats that were borrowed from Blake's 7.

(170) Matt Smith had a beautiful new TARDIS interior when he became the Doctor but it was later changed to a more functional 'machine' like design. Steven Moffat said they changed it because the original 'whimsical' interior was very difficult to film in.

(171) Doctor Who: Flux consisted of six episodes. Doctor Who was in serious trouble around this time due to the pandemic and budget cuts. Chris Chibnall said the show was actually axed at one point and he and Jodi Whittaker were offered other work. They decided though to stick with Doctor Who and managed to get the go ahead for Flux. To the credit of Chibnall, despite all the problems, he reacted by trying to do something ambitious in telling one big story. And this was

surely playing to his strengths too because Chibnall's long form story work on Broadchurch was a lot better than his episodic work on Doctor Who.

(172) Though some fans (though obviously not all) were hoping Chris Chibnall's Timeless Child backstory would be overturned or simply ignored by the next showrunner this was unrealistic because Russell T Davies is obviously a friend of Chibnall and he was not going to brush Chibnall's big concept under the carpet and pretend it never happened.

(173) Dr Who and the Daleks is a film that fans of the television show sometimes tend to be a little on the sniffy side about whenever it rears its head in conversation. This is mostly because it is not canon and so therefore can never be a true part of the history of the character. It would be fun to see the television show do an episode where they somehow made Cushing's Doctor canon! Maybe he lost his memory and thought he was human?

(174) The Sontarans are a warrior race bent on conquest and are known for their militaristic nature and their distinctive appearance, which includes large, bulky bodies and dome-potato shaped heads.

(175) Russell T Davies is often referred to as 'RTD' in Doctor Who fandom.

(176) The Carry On star Jim Dale was considered for the Fourth Doctor.

(177) Steven Moffat said he got the idea to cast Peter Capaldi as the Doctor because he kept bumping into Peter in BBC corridors late at night!

(178) The talented Irish actor Cyril Cusack turned down an offer to become the first ever Doctor when the show started.

(179) K-9 was apparently a nightmare to operate because it would keep stopping and bump into things.

(180) Tom Baker, Ian Marter, James Hill wrote a screenplay for a proposed Doctor Who feature film called Doctor Who Meets Scratchman in the late 1970s. However, funding for the film was a big obstacle and with the release of Star Wars they decided to abandon the project.

(181) Jon Pertwee's Third Doctor era owes something to The Avengers, James Bond, and Adam Adamant. Pertwee's Doctor is more of a dandy and more of an action hero than the two Doctors who came before him.

(182) 1966's Daleks' Invasion Earth 2150 A.D. is the second and last of the Amicus Doctor Who films and was again directed by Gordon Flemyng and written by Milton Subotsky (though it seems that David Whitaker once again worked on the screenplay and was likely the real author).

(183) The story in Daleks' Invasion Earth 2150 A.D. is based on the Doctor Who television serial The Dalek Invasion of Earth. Peter Cushing and Roberta Tovey reprise their roles as the Doctor and his granddaughter Susan respectively.

(184) Peter Cushing apparently said he would only do Invasion Earth 2150 A.D. if they asked Roberta Tovey to come back too - which was a very sweet gesture on his part.

(185) William Russell appeared as Ian Chesterton in the 2022 special The Power of the Doctor. William's last appearance in the show had been way back in 1965.

(186) Janet Fielding is an Australian actress who played companion Tegan Jovanka from 1981 to 1984. At a 1993 comic con event, Fielding complained that women were not treated well on the show. She also blamed the show for killing her acting career (she only appeared in a few bit part roles after Doctor Who). Fielding later became a theatrical agent.

(187) Despite her past issues with Doctor Who, Janet Fielding did later do some Big Finish stories as Tegan and also played Tegan in The Power of the Doctor (Jodie's last episode as the Thirteenth Doctor).

(188) The legendary comedian Ken Dodd appeared in Delta and the Bannermen as The Tollmaster.

(189) Bob Monkhouse was supposed to play The Tollmaster in Delta and the Bannermen but in the end he was too busy and couldn't do it.

(190) World Enough and Time was written by Steven Moffat and directed by Rachel Talalay. This is one of the most acclaimed episodes of Doctor Who since the show returned in 2005 and also one of the creepiest. The premise has the Doctor (Peter Capaldi) answering a distress call from a huge spaceship being sucked into a black hole. The Doctor though is 'training' Missy (Michelle Gomez) - the evil Time Lord - to be good and trusts her to be in charge of this adventure. That turns out to be a very big mistake.

There are a lot of enjoyable horror elements in this episode and plenty of shocks. The Doctor's companion Bill (Pearl Mackie) is shot early on and we get a shocking moment where she looks down and sees that a hole has literally been blasted through her body. World Enough and Time brings back the Mondasian Cybermen - who are basically Cybermen but with bandages wrapped around their faces and weird distorted voices. The story gets full value out of the creep factor of these robotic aliens. Bill is resurrected by the Cybermen and taken to the other side of the ship which - lest we forget - is trapped in a black hole. So time is affected. To the Doctor it may only seem like minutes to get to Bill, for Bill it is years. The scenes of Bill at the other side of the ship are enjoyably hellish and dystopian with bandaged hospital patients who only seem to say "pain!" in eerie distorted voices. She strikes up a sort of friendship with a strange character who turns to be (spoiler) John Simm's Master in disguise. This is one of the big reveals at the end. The Master is back and seemingly now in cohorts with his future incarnation Missy.

The other big reveal is that Bill has been converted into a Mondasian Cyberman. This is a shocking moment of body horror and supplies yet another grisly twist to an episode that has been chock full of them. World Enough and Time is Doctor Who at or around its very best and plays like a skewed Twilight Zone episode with impressive production design and an escalating aura of dread and unease. It is already considered to be one of the classic episodes of Doctor Who in any era.

(191) Torchwood is an anagram of Doctor Who.

(192) One of the most infamous Doctor Who interviews occurred when Benjamin Cook (for Doctor Who magazine) interviewed the veteran actor Clive Swift in 2008 about his role as Mr Copper in Voyage of the Damned. Swift seemed highly irritable during the interview, calling one question 'stupid', and even stated that Doctor Who wasn't a big deal. Most fans seem to find this grumpy interview quite amusing!

(193) Doctor Who was banned in China because the regime

there decided that time travel as a concept was a frivolous rewriting of history!

(194) Jenna Coleman began her acting career in the soap opera Emmerdale.

(195) Sally Sparrow, the heroine of Blink, was earmarked as a permanent companion but this plan was scuppered because Carey Mulligan had no interest being in a regular role on Doctor Who. Mulligan went on to become a pretty big film star. She did say though that she is proud of being a part of Doctor Who history and wouldn't mind revisiting Sally one day.

(196) Jon Pertwee said the Draconians were his favourite Doctor Who monster.

(197) Though it has its fans, the Chris Chibnall era of Doctor Who is generally seen as one of the weakest eras in the show's history. Some feel that the Chibnall era did lasting damage to the franchise.

(198) Steven Moffat said Peter Calpaldi played the Doctor in a more abrasive way in his first season than he had expected. Capaldi's Doctor did soften somewhat in the end and become a bit warmer.

(199) Chris Jury is often said to have been considered for the part of the Seventh Doctor before Sylvester McCoy was cast. Jury is best known as the bumbling Eric Catchpole in Lovejoy. Jury has since said though that he is unaware that he was in contention to play the Doctor. He was of course in The Greatest Show in the Galaxy.

(200) Robert Holmes said he disliked historical Doctor Who

stories where the Doctor meets a real figure from history. He much preferred aliens and horror yarns.

(201) Alan Webb declined an offer to replace William Hartnell as the Doctor because he didn't want to commit to a television series. Webb is an English actor who later appeared in films like The Great Train Robbery and The Duellists.

(202) Dr Who and the Daleks is unashamedly a film for children. The television show is also aimed at children but it has references, jokes, and horror elements that give it a broader appeal too. The television show is frequently much darker and more melodramatic than the Amicus films based on this iconic property. Dr Who and the Daleks is much more family friendly and undemanding than the television source.

(203) Steven Moffat said he cast Jenna Coleman as the companion because she was one of the few people in the auditions who could talk fast enough to keep up with Matt Smith!

(204) Chris Chibnall said his Timeless Child arc was based on him being adopted.

(205) The lowest rated episode of NuWho on IMDB is Orphan 55 with a dismal 4.2 out of ten.

(206) Simon Pegg was supposed to play Rose Tyler's father but he couldn't do it in the end because he became unavailable - though he did still appear in Doctor Who.

(207) Nicola Bryant said she didn't much enjoy Peri wearing skimpy clothes and shorts. She felt (not unreasonably) that this was purely designed to boost ratings.

(208) Richard Hurndall said that playing the First Doctor in The Five Doctors was made easier by the fact that he'd worked with Jon Pertwee and Patrick Troughton before in other things.

(209) They planned to make a trilogy of the Amicus Doctor Who films but Daleks' Invasion Earth 2150 A.D. turned out to be the last outing for Peter Cushing's Doctor. The box-office returns of Daleks' Invasion Earth 2150 A.D. (which had a bigger budget than the first film) were not deemed sufficient to do another one. It appears that the public demand for more big screen Dalek capers was already waning and so Amicus decided to get out of the Doctor Who racket.

(210) Daleks' Invasion Earth 2150 A.D. is largely more of the same that you got with Dr Who and the Daleks. If you didn't like the first one then this second slice of Amicus Dr Who probably won't convert you but if you did enjoy the original you might actually like this sequel more. This film is more eventful and action packed and the plot is more fun. It's just as colourful as the first film and the special effects are better too. The flying saucer in the film especially is really good and quite eerie too. If you love old school special effects with models and miniatures you'll have a lot of fun with Daleks' Invasion Earth 2150 A.D.

(211) The Abzorbaloff (played by Peter Kaye) in Love & Monsters was the result of a Blue Peter competition in which viewers designed their own alien monster.

(212) It was often presumed that Doctor Who post 2005 was under a contractual obligation to use the Daleks in each season under the terms of an agreement with the estate of Terry Nation. Steven Moffat has said though that this wasn't true.

(213) Christopher Eccleston departed from NuWho after just one series. His departure was known even as the series aired. He said he didn't like the 'culture' and 'environment' of the production. Eccleston has been pretty scathing of Russell T Davies in more recent years.

(214) April Walker was originally cast as Sarah Jane Smith and began shooting but she was later replaced by Elisabeth Sladen. It was Jon Pertwee who asked for Walker to be replaced. His main complaint was that she was too tall. April Walker has been in many things but is probably best known for The Wedding Party episode of Fawlty Towers.

(215) April Walker, due to a non disclosure agreement, was only able to talk about being axed from Doctor Who many years later. She said she was very annoyed at Jon Pertwee pushing her off the show.

(216) The Master was designed to be Moriarty to the Doctor's Sherlock Holmes.

(217) The Deadly Assassin was inspired by The Manchurian Candidate.

(218) It was proposed that the model and actress Twiggy would have been the Doctor's companion in Doctor Who Meets Scratchman had it been made.

(219) Patrick Troughton said he tried to make his Doctor completely different from the First Doctor because it would have been pointless to try and copy Bill Hartnell.

(220) Jon Pertwee said one of the reasons he left Doctor Who was because he was saddened by the death of his friend and co-star Roger Delgado.

(221) Russell T Davies got his start in children's television. He worked on shows like Play School and Why Don't You?

(222) River Song is a recurring character who has a complex relationship with the Doctor, as her timeline is often out of sync with his.

(223) Russell T Davies said the 2024 episode Dot and Bubble was an idea he had many years ago but was impossible to make during his first run on the show because it needed too many special effects.

(224) Billie Piper was a popular suggestion to be the new companion when Doctor Who was brought back in 2005 and so it was perhaps no surprise when she was cast as Rose. Piper had a fairly short lived pop career before transitioning into acting.

(225) Torchwood is a spin-off of Doctor Who and follows the adventures of a team of alien investigators based in Cardiff, Wales. The team, led by the enigmatic Captain Jack Harkness, investigates and fights against extraterrestrial threats while also dealing with their own personal demons and complex relationships. The show was known for its darker and more mature themes compared to Doctor Who and has gained a dedicated fanbase. Russell T Davies and Chris Chibnall both worked on Torchwood.

(226) The BBC implied that Christopher Eccleston left Doctor Who because he feared becoming typecast but this wasn't true and they later had to retract that comment.

(227) The Fifth Doctor's cricket jumper was suggested by Peter Davison.

(228) David Tennant's Doctor was supposed to wear boots but Tennant insisted on Converse trainers instead.

(229) On 24 September 2021, to the surprise of Doctor Who fans, it was announced that Russell T Davies would be returning to the show to replace Chris Chibnall as showrunner. Davies had once said he would never write another Doctor Who story so he'd obviously done an about turn about this. It would probably be fair to say his second tenure as showrunner has been a mixed bag thus far and hasn't managed to replicate the success of his first tenure.

(230) Terry Nation died in Los Angeles in 1997. One of the last things he worked on as a writer was the action show MacGyver.

(231) Adric was a companion of the Fourth and Fifth Doctors, portrayed by actor Matthew Waterhouse. Adric was a brilliant mathematician from the planet Alzarius and was part of a group of survivors who were brought on board the TARDIS by the Fourth Doctor. Adric had a complex relationship with the Doctor and his fellow companions, often questioning their decisions and motives. He ultimately sacrificed himself to save the universe in the serial Earthshock.

(232) Christopher Eccleston was the most plainly dressed Doctor we've ever had. He simply wore a medium length leather jacket. Eccleston said this was intentional because he wanted the 'flamboyance' to come from his acting rather than the costume.

(233) Steven Moffat made a surprise return to Doctor Who in 2024 to write the episode Boom and also the Christmas special for the end of the year.

(234) The Christmas special Voyage Of the Damned, which guest starred Kylie Minogue, got an incredible 13.3 million viewers in Britain.

(235) Blake's 7 star Jacqueline Pearce appeared in the Colin Baker era story The Two Doctors. Jacqueline Pearce said she'd never actually watched a single episode of Doctor Who in her life when she appeared in this.

(236) Hugh Grant was considered for the Doctor when the show came back in 2005. A script was sent to him but his agent didn't pass it on because he presumed Grant wouldn't be interested.

(237) Michael Grade said he felt that Doctor Who had run its course by the late 1980s and needed a long rest. He also felt the series had become too violent for a teatime kids show. Critics of Michael Grade's decision argued that merchandise revenue from the show still made it viable but Grade felt the show simply wasn't cost effective for the BBC to make anymore.

(238) The Devil's Chord ended with a big musical number. It is probably fair to say that this was not to all tastes.

(239) Once established in the role, William Hartnell was paid £315 an episode on Doctor Who.

(240) Bernard Padden, who played Tylos in the 1980 story Full Circle, was considered for the part of Adric.

(241) Dr Who and the Daleks is very much of a product of its time with the jazzy sixties atmosphere (the Thals look like beatniks with their pudding bowl haircuts and waistcoats) and Cushing's rather avuncular doddery grandfather Doctor a

long way removed from the character we've seen in the television show over the decades. If you aren't too obsessed though about the continuity of Doctor Who or expecting 2001: A Space Odyssey, then Dr Who and the Daleks is actually quite good fun. The eye popping colour of the film is enjoyable (especially from a modern vantage point where films often look dark and grainy) and there are some decent sets and designs too.

(242) Jon Pertwee was the first Doctor to have colour episodes.

(243) Matt Smith said playing the Doctor was the hardest role he's ever played because there were so many lines to learn.

(244) David Fielder auditioned for the part of the Seventh Doctor before Sylvester McCoy was cast. Fielder is a stage actor who has also been in things like Superman III and Heartbeat. He seemed to take a long hiatus from acting at one point in the 1990s.

(245) One slightly odd thing is that the two Amicus Doctor Who films still remain the only two big screen adventures for this iconic character. For some reason no one has since made a Doctor Who feature film purely for cinemas - which is strange when you think about it. In the 1970s literally everything on British television got a big screen spin-off film - from On the Buses to Doomwatch to The Sweeney to For the Love of Ada. But there was no Doctor Who film.

(246) Sophie Aldred caused a mild rumpus as Ace at first because she didn't have shaved armpits. Sophie was told to shave them after this.

(247) The legendary producer Verity Lambert worked on the first couple of years of Doctor who. Not only was she the

youngest ever producer at the time she was also the only female producer so something of a trailblazer.

(248) The Doctor's TARDIS has a mind of its own and sometimes takes the Doctor where he needs to go, rather than where he wants to go.

(249) Karen Gillan auditioned to play a companion (who had not yet been named Amy Pond) with both an English and Scottish accent. In the end they let Karen play the part with her Scottish accent.

(250) Planet of the Spiders was no picnic for Elisabeth Sladen because she was scared of spiders.

(251) The 1966 film Daleks' Invasion Earth 2150 A.D. has a new comic relief companion as Roy Castle is replaced by Bernard Cribbins as a policeman named Tom Campbell. Tom ends up in the TARDIS when he mistakes it for a real police box. Bernard would play Wilf Mott many years later in the television show.

(252) Patrick Troughton said he was hesitant to accept the part of the Second Doctor at first because he presumed the show was on the way out and wouldn't last much longer without William Hartnell.

(253) Frazier Hines said he was paid £64 an episode to play the Second Doctor's companion. £64 was obviously a lot more money in those days than it is today.

(254) The show went out on Sunday when Chris Chibnall was in charge - which didn't feel right. Doctor Who doesn't feel like a Sunday evening show. It feels like a loss of prestige to move from Saturday.

(255) In the Chibnall era the show also lost its Christmas Day slot. The traditional festive special went out on New Year's Eve under Chibnall. Russell T Davies returned Doctor Who to Saturday and Christmas Day when he replaced Chibnall as showrunner.

(256) John Barrowman as Captain Jack finally returned to the show in the Chibnall era episode Fugitive of the Judoon. Chris Chibnall did an excellent job of keeping this secret and thus making Jack's return a nice surprise for viewers.

(257) There's a nice theme in Nikola Tesla's Night of Terror where Tesla and the Doctor bond because they have much in common. Both are outsiders, scientists, and inventors. Both are considered eccentric. Tesla was Serbian and so sometimes felt as if it was more difficult for him to be accepted in America. Nikola Tesla's Night of Terror has an obvious subtext about the positive contribution that immigrants can make to a society.

(258) In the episode Can You Hear Me?, the Thirteenth Doctor sort of blanks Graham when he tries to talk about his cancer. This scene drew some criticism and the BBC even received complaints.

(259) The Doctor's real name has never been revealed in the series.

(260) In the episode The Brain of Morbius, there is a scene where Elisabeth Sladen calls the Doctor by the name 'Tom'. No one must have spotted this blooper because it was left in.

(261) Anthony Head tested to play the Doctor for the 1996 television film. Head is best known the television show Buffy the Vampire Slayer.

(262) Tecteun is the Doctor's adoptive mother in Chris Chibnall's new version of the Doctor's origins. Barbara Flynn played this character.

(263) Rupert Davies was approached to play the Second Doctor but he wasn't interested. Davies was best known for playing Maigret in the 1960s.

(264) The most memorable scenes in The Power of the Doctor come when Ace and Tegan meet their respective Doctors (or holographic versions of them anyway) again. Sylvester McCoy in particular is great in his scene with Sophie Aldred. The sequence where Jodie's Doctor meets these morphing versions of her former self is also wonderfully done.

(265) Peter Davison suffered for his art in Warriors of the Deep because he had to plunge into freezing cold water.

(266) Colin Baker's first story as the Doctor was The Twin Dilemma. The Twin Dilemma is considered by many fans to be the nadir of Classic Who and the beginning of the end for the show.

(267) Many people love the 1970s era of Classic Who the most because the gothic, Hammer and folk horror influences are often very apparent.

(268) Davros is a brilliant scientist but also a megalomaniacal dictator.

(269) When the show was axed by Michael Grade in the late 1980s it was still getting live viewing figures of several million. While the current version of Doctor Who would kill for overnights like that, these were not amazing figures for the late 1980s because there were only four channels and

streaming and the internet was still in the future.

(270) Nikola Tesla's Night of Terror features Anjli Mohindra - who was of course Rani Chandra in The Sarah Jane Adventures. Mohindra is the chief baddie - Queen of the Skithra. This character is so similar to the Racnoss Empress from the David Tennant era that everyone presumed it would be the same alien.

(271) It was initially speculated that Jo Martin's 'Fugitive' Doctor was a Doctor from an alternate universe but Chris Chibnall debunked this theory and insisted that Ruth is a real Doctor.

(272) There was speculation that Praxeus was going to be a Sea Devils episode but that obviously didn't transpire in the end.

(273) Bonnie Langford began her career as a child actor. She was in things like Bugsy Malone, Wombling Free, and Just William.

(274) Christopher Eccleston said he never watched Doctor Who as a child.

(275) Peter Capaldi on the other hand was a big Doctor Who fan when he was growing up.

(276) Catherine Tate said she was amazed to become a Doctor Who companion. Because she was primarily a comedian she didn't think she'd get such a big acting gig.

(277) William Hartnell wore a wig when he played the Doctor because he had short hair in real life.

(278) There was a lot of fan speculation that Jon Pertwee's actor son Sean was going to be in Empire of Death playing the Third Doctor but this obviously never happened.

(279) Village of the Angels is one of the brights spots of the Chibnall era. In this episode, the Doctor, Yaz, and Dan find themselves trapped in the spooky mist hazed village of Medderton in 1967. Yaz and Dan join the search for a missing girl named Peggy while the Doctor chances upon a Professor Jericho (Kevin McNally) - who is conducting psychic research on Claire. Claire is the women who recognised the Doctor in the first part of Flux. This mystery all revolves around a rogue Weeping Angel - which will spell big trouble and peril for the Doctor, Claire, and Jericho.

Village of the Angels has a terrific sense of atmosphere and essentially becomes a siege episode in the end when the Angels seek to get into Professor Jericho's lab. There is a real sense of danger for the Doctor, Claire, and Jericho in this episode and we feel that danger too because the characters are well developed. It helps a lot that you have an old pro like Kevin McNally as Jericho and by the end of the episode McNally has made us care enough about Professor Jericho to want him to survive.

(280) Colin Baker was a huge fan of Doctor Who when he got the part. He'd watched it right from the beginning.

(281) After she moved out of acting, Janet Fielding was actually Paul McGann's agent at one point.

(282) Robert Holmes, who was one of the most celebrated writers on the show, said that he took great delight in scaring children with his stories!

(283) What made Chris Chibnall most attractive to the BBC as the Doctor Who showrunner was his work as the creator and lead writer on the ITV drama Broadchurch. Chibnall was seen as a safe pair of hands. He was an experienced television writer and showrunner. Plus, he was a lifelong Doctor Who fan. What could possibly go wrong? The doubts - as far as Doctor Who fans were concerned - came from the previous episodes of Doctor Who that Chibnall had written. 42, The Hungry Earth/Cold Blood, Dinosaurs on a Spaceship, The Power of Three. None of these episodes were especially memorable.

(284) The premise of Daleks' Invasion Earth 2150 A.D. has the TARDIS shuttling through time and space again and ending up in the year 2150 where it transpires that the Daleks have invaded Earth. The Daleks have started turning humans into brainwashed 'Robomen' and England seems to be a pile of rubble ruled over by its deadly new pepperpot masters. The Daleks are intent on using the Earth's core to create a giant spaceship and - as ever - it will be to the Doctor and his plucky companions to put a stop to their nefarious plans.

(285) Blake Harrison has a guest spot in Village of the Angels and has a lot more luck than his old Inbetweeners co-star James Buckley. Harrison got Village of the Angels while poor old James Buckley was in Orphan 55!

(286) Tom Baker was so unimpressed by the acting of Matthew Waterhouse as Adric that he suggested the character should be a mute!

(287) The second highest rated episode of NuWho on IMDB is Heaven Sent with a rating of 9.6 out of ten.

(288) Ella Road, who co-wrote the terrible Chibnall era episode

Legend of the Sea Devils, was once called Britain's most promising playwright. Heaven knows what Ella Road must have thought when she watched Legend of the Sea Devils!

(289) It seems that Chris Chibnall overeached himself in the end with the Flux episodes and couldn't quite make a smooth landing after a very promising beginning. You have to give him a lot of credit for trying though. It is admirable that he put together this big bold crazy story arc and managed to get it produced at a time when things were exceptionally difficult for the television industry and the future of Doctor Who was by no means certain.

(290) Patrick Troughton and Frazier Hines returned as the Doctor and Jamie in the Colin Baker episode The Two Doctors. It is never explained why the Second Doctor and Jamie look much older than they used to!

(291) Orphan 55 had some production issues by all accounts and boy does it show. This episode feels unfinished and rushed.

(292) Showrunner is basically a fancy term for head producer.

(293) The series twelve finale The Timeless Children drew only 4.6 million viewers - at the time the worst figures since the show came back in 2005.

(294) When she became the first female Doctor, Jodie Whittaker said her gender was not relevant because the Doctor is an alien and not defined by human definitions like gender.

(295) Graham Crowden was considered for the part of the Fourth Doctor but he was only willing to commit to one series

so had to be ruled out. He later played Soldeed in The Horns of Nimon.

(296) It is sometimes reported that Michelle Ryan auditioned to become the permanent companion after Billie Piper left but Ryan has said this isn't true.

(297) Eric Saward, a script editor on Doctor Who under John Nathan Turner, was famously scathing of his former boss in a Starburst interview. Saward lambasted JNT for hiring 'novice' writers and bad directors. He also complained that JNT had been impossible to arrange a meeting with because he kept jetting off to American fan conventions.

(298) William Hartnell relished the part of the Doctor because at the time he was becoming typecast in stern military roles.

(299) Listen is a superb brooding 2014 episode of Doctor Who directed by Douglas Mackinnon. The Doctor (Peter Capaldi) wonders why people have a recurring dream of a hand grabbing their foot from under the bed. His musings take him from a spooky children's home in the past to the end of time in the far future. Listen uses a simple premise to great effect. The 'monster' in this episode is unseen and might not even exist. It's the thing under the bed or behind the door. The episode is about how we cope with fear and generates a wonderful sense of unease. The story takes us to a surprising place in the end and Steven Moffat's script does a nice job in bringing everything together and making all those little moments reward the observant viewer who has been paying attention.

(300) Before the casting of Jodie Whittaker, other names floated in speculation included Tilda Swinton, Sheridan Smith, Hayley Attwell, and Gemma Whelan. Nothing ever

came of the Swinton speculation while Smith, one of the most acclaimed actresses on British television, was simply too busy to nail herself down to one part. Hayley Attwell was a popular fan suggestion and would obviously have made a dashing and charismatic Doctor.

(301) Sylvester McCoy's Doctor makes a brief appearance in the 1996 television movie but quickly makes way for the Eighth Doctor.

(302) Millie Gibson was most famous for Coronation Street when she joined Doctor Who. Russell T Davies is a big soap fan.

(303) Noel Clarke, who played Mickey Smith, said he was a bit confused appearing in Doctor Who at first when it came back in 2005 because he had no idea what the tone of it was supposed to be. He said he had no idea if he was supposed to be playing this straight or if the show was a comedy spoof.

(304) The Canadian Broadcasting Corporation considered dubbing the Doctor when the show came back in 2005 because they didn't think Canadian viewers would understand Christopher Eccleston's northern English accent.

(305) Rose was supposed to fake a Scottish accent in Tooth and Claw but they scrapped this plan because Billie Piper's attempted Scottish accent was so awful.

(306) In the first part of Spyfall, Stephen Fry's C assumes that Bradley Walsh's Graham is the Doctor at first and he won't be the last person in series twelve to make this mistake. This even led to a fan theory that Graham was really a Doctor who had lost his memory!

(307) David Tennant said he gave his Doctor spectacles because he thought this would be nice for children who wear glasses to see that the Doctor was like them.

(308) Peter Kay turned down the part of Elton in Love & Monsters because he wanted to play the villain.

(309) The episode Fear Her revolves around the (then) forthcoming London Olympics. This unavoidably makes the episode rather dated today.

(310) A Chibnall era villain is Tzim-Sha (Samuel Oatley) of the warlike Stenza. The Stenza are patently inspired by Stan Winston's Predator. They are intergalactic hunters who collect the teeth of their victims to decorate their faces.

(311) Laura Fraser, who played Lydia Rodarte-Quayle in Breaking Bad and Better Call Saul, was a guest star in Orphan 55. It's a shame they couldn't have found a better episode for her to appear in!

(312) The Fires of Pompeii used some of the same sets as the HBO show Rome.

(313) The Face of Boe is a large, enigmatic character. It is a humanoid head that is said to be the oldest living being in the universe. The Face of Boe is known for its wisdom and mysterious abilities, and it often serves as a wise mentor to the Doctor and his companions. Its true origins and nature remain shrouded in mystery.

(314) Russell T Davies has never confirmed if Captain Jack really is the Face of Boe.

(315) Tommy Knight, who played Luke Smith in The Sarah

Jane Adventures and Doctor Who, doesn't seem to act anymore and is now a computer coder.

(316) Tom Baker said he was very touched and proud that his Doctor was a hero to many children.

(317) Robert Holmes passed away while working on the Colin Baker story The Ultimate Foe.

(318) Jon Pertwee had trouble with some of the scientific babble the Doctor had to say so it was sometimes written on cards around the set for him to read.

(319) Tom Baker said the end of Doctor Who Meets Scratchman would have had the Doctor trapped in a giant pinball machine!

(320) Patrick Troughton's Doctor was supposed to have a curly wig but the producers decided they didn't like this idea and gave him a Beatles hairstyle instead. That sort of hairstyle had gone out of date by then but it was perfect for the Doctor - who is very much a man always slightly out of time.

(321) Despite playing Jamie in Doctor Who, Frazer Hines in from Yorkshire in real life although he did have a Scottish mother.

(322) The Invisible Enemy was heavily inspired by the film Fantastic Voyage.

(323) The Doctor has a complicated relationship with the Time Lords, his own people, who often view him with suspicion and distrust.

(324) Georgia Moffett, who later played the Doctor's cloned

daughter (and married to David Tennant in real life), lobbied for the part of Rose Tyler but was told she looked too young.

(325) Matt Smith auditioned to play Dr Watson in Steven Moffat's show Sherlock. Smith was deemed too eccentric to be a good foil for Benedict Cumberbatch but Moffat clearly took note of Smith because he cast him as the lead in Doctor Who. Matt Smith seemed more like a Sherlock Holmes than a Dr Watson.

(326) Dermot Crowley auditioned for the part of the Seventh Doctor before Sylvester McCoy was cast. Dermot Crowley is an Irish stage actor with many film and television credits. He did a very interesting audition but it wasn't quite what they were looking for.

(327) The Thirteenth Doctor's clothes reminded some of the outfits Robin Williams used to wear in the sitcom Mork & Mindy.

(328) The very talented Ron Moody turned down an approach to become the Third Doctor. Moody later said that was one of his biggest acting regrets and mistakes.

(329) It is probably fair to say that 80s Doctor Who struggled to replace Tom Baker. He left shoes too big to be filled.

(330) Christopher Eccleston claimed in an interview that the BBC blacklisted him after he left Doctor Who so he had to go to America and work over there - which he didn't much enjoy.

(331) David Tennant's last episode (in his original run, when he turns into Matt Smith) actually beat Coronation Street in the ratings.

(332) Billy Connolly was on a shortlist to play the Doctor in the 1996 TV movie. Connolly later said he was a big Doctor Who fan and would loved to have done it but no one approached him to discuss the role.

(333) Look out for Ray Brooks in Daleks' Invasion Earth 2150 A.D. as a resistance leader. Brooks was coming off the success of The Knack ...and How to Get It - which was directed by Richard Lester.

(334) Rusell Tovey auditioned to become the Eleventh Doctor but lost out to Matt Smith. Tovey later said he would have found the role and the fame too overwhelming had he been cast.

(335) Before he was cast the Doctor, David Tennant had worked with Russell T Davies on the Casanova adaptation. Davies had clearly seen Doctor potential in Tennant and therefore had an 'oven ready' replacement for Christopher Eccleston up his sleeve.

(336) Murray Gold, the Chibnall era aside, has been the composer on NuWho since it came back. Gold has written some brilliant and stirring themes for the show but he is sometimes criticised for drowning out the action and not realising that less can sometimes be more.

(337) William Hartnell and Peter Capaldi were both 55 when they started playing the Doctor - making them the joint oldest actors to win the part.

(338) The episode Rosa in the Chris Chibnall era was actually shot in South Africa despite being set in the United States.

(339) Steven Moffat once said that the central concept of

Doctor Who is so strong that the show can even survive 'not being done very well'.

(340) The Legend of Ruby Sunday has the lowest live BBC viewing figures in Doctor Who history.

(341) Nicola Bryant said a lot of people thought she was American in real life.

(342) Although he returned as the Eighth Doctor in a mini episode and in The Power of the Doctor, Paul McGann said he has never actually watched Doctor Who. He loved playing the Doctor but it wasn't a show he watched at home.

(343) The Tenth Doctor's catchphrase was "Allons-y!" which is French for "Let's go!"

(344) Hugh Futcher, who played Hickman in The Sea Devils, was considered for the part of the Seventh Doctor when Colin Baker was fired. Futcher appeared in several Carry On films and many television shows. He was also in the classic horror films Repulsion and Quatermass and the Pit.

(345) Despite being set in the year 2150, the buildings and vehicles in Daleks' Invasion Earth 2150 A.D. all look very 1950s and 1960s!

(346) Steven Moffat said that one of the reasons he cast Peter Capaldi is that we'd just had two young Doctors in Tennant and Smith and so he felt it was time to do something different and cast a more mature actor.

(347) When he left the role of the Doctor, Tom Baker dropped some hints that his successor might be female. This was a publicity stunt designed to generate interest in the show. We

did though of course get the first female Doctor in the end under Chris Chibnall.

(348) Alan Cumming said he turned down an approach to play the Doctor a couple of times because he didn't want to relocate from New York to Cardiff. Cumming later turned up as King James in The Witchfinders.

(349) Matt Smith's career stuttered a bit after he left Doctor Who (his scenes in a Terminator sequel famously hit the cutting room floor) but thanks to The Crown and House of the Dragon he seems to be going from strength to strength.

(350) Stratford Johns was approached to play the Third Doctor but declined to pursue the role. He later appeared in the show in Four to Doomsday.

(351) Peter Davison was a big fan of Doctor Who before he was cast and remembered watching the show as a youngster.

(352) The Canadian actress Katie Boland was the original choice for Ashildr but she had visa issues and was replaced by Maisie Williams.

(353) Michael Crawford was considered for the part of the Doctor in the 1996 television film.

(354) Frazer Hines joined the cast of the soap opera Emmerdale Farm (later simply called Emmerdale) when he left Doctor Who. Frazer was in over 1,500 episodes of Emmerdale!

(355) Paul McGann's Eighth Doctor returned in The Night of the Doctor mini-episode and also appeared in Jodie Whittaker's farewell episode The Power of the Doctor. Many

fans liked the idea of doing an Eighth Doctor spin-off season with McGann but sadly it never happened in the end and seems unlikely to do so.

(356) K-9 is an intelligent and loyal robot dog, equipped with a laser weapon and various other useful gadgets. He has appeared in various episodes and spin-off media throughout the history of the show, and is known for his dry wit and mechanical charm.

(357) Russell T Davies said that during his first era in charge of running Doctor Who the BBC wanted to do a CBBC spin-off show featuring the Doctor as a young boy. Russell thought this was a dreadful idea and persuaded them to do Sarah Jane Adventures instead.

(358) The 1971 story The Dæmons is clearly inspired by Quatermass And The Pit - a Nigel Kneale story which was adapted for both television and film. A strange skull is discovered by workmen in London and further excavation unearths what appears to be an unexploded bomb. However, on closer inspection, the bomb turns out to be an alien spacecraft containing not only alien bodies but a strange psychic energy and poltergeists. Professor Bernard Quatermass of the British Rocket Group investigates the mystery as danger beckons for all of us. Quatermass And The Pit works on so many levels that it's not difficult to see why the story - and Kneale - are so influential and lauded. It's a horror detective story, a sci-fi mystery, a ghost story, a witchcraft tale involving aliens, and Kneale also works in some topical references to race riots.

(359) A huge and elaborate new TARDIS interior was built for the second Russell T Davies era and introduced at the end of The Star Beast with David Tennant. Oddly though, we rarely

see this swanky new TARDIS interior in the 2024 series with Ncuti Gatwa that followed!

(360) When we got the 60th anniversary specials with Russell T Davies they were largely enjoyable (if not perfect) but the one disappointing thing is that they didn't really feel like anniversary specials or celebrations of Who. They just felt like some extra bonus episodes with Tennant and Catherine Tate.

(361) Janet Fielding said she was delighted to have a fairly large role as Tegan in The Power of the Doctor because she'd assumed it would just be a cameo.

(362) Village of the Angels is the fourth part of the Flux arc and one of the best episodes of the Chibnall era. Like the season twelve episode The Haunting of Villa Diodati, it was co-written by Chibnall and Maxine Alderton. It's a shame really that Maxine Alderton didn't do a lot more writing on Doctor Who during the Chibnall era because the quality of the show seemed to suddenly improve whenever her name was on a script. One might argue that Maxine Alderton would be a better lead writer for the show than Chibnall or Davies!

(363) One strange thing about the promotion of series twelve was the way that at the half-way point, the promotional strategy seemed intent on reminding people that we only had a few episodes to go until the big finale. While it was fine to drum up early interest in the two-part finale this strategy didn't seem to express much confidence in Praxeus and Can You Hear Me? at all!

(364) Nicola Bryant became a big sex symbol through playing Peri. She got hundreds of fan letters each week when she was on Doctor Who.

(365) The Thirteenth Doctor's companions Graham and Ryan departed in Revolution of the Daleks. Graham did return though for Thirteen's last episode.

(366) When the show came back in 2005, Russell T Davies strongly considered Martin Clunes for the part of the Doctor. Clunes is best known for Doc Martin and Men Behaving Badly.

(367) Colin Baker refused to film his regeneration sequence because he had been fired on the orders of Michael Grade. Colin said that what irritated him the most was that he never got an explanation for why he been fired.

(368) In The Power of the Doctor, just for a change, the Doctor regenerates on a cliff by the sea rather than inside an exploding TARDIS. It's something different and makes for a lovely shot with Segun Akinola's epic music.

(369) The Toymaker dancing to The Spice Girls in The Giggle was perhaps inspired by the Master and the Rasputin song in The Power of the Doctor. Russell T Davies had shown a fondness for musical scenes before though with John Simm's Master.

(370) Legend of the Sea Devils was supposed to be part of a series thirteen which events nixed. When it finally went into production it was hobbled by the pandemic and also a script that plainly needed more work.

(371) We see the Doctor playing cricket in Black Orchid. Peter Davison was a handy cricketer himself in real life.

(372) Jon Pertwee's most famous role after Doctor Who was as Worzel Gummidge. Worzel Gummidge was a children's drama/comedy that began in 1979. The series was based on

the Worzel Gummidge books by Barbara Euphan Todd. Worzel Gummidge is a scarecrow on Scatterbrook Farm. Worzel is no ordinary scarecrow though. He was created by the mysterious Crowman (Geoffrey Bayldon) and it seems that the Crowman's creations were given the gift of life. So daft old Worzel frequently comes to life when no one is around and gets into all manner of comical scrapes. The only people who seem to know he's real are the two children on the farm. Worzel has two all consuming passions. The pursuit of the snooty coconut shy doll Aunt Sally (Una Stubbs) and his great love of cake.

(373) Quantum Leap and Star Trek star Scott Bakula turned down the part of Isaac in the Matt Smith episode A Town Called Mercy because of other commitments. Bakula said that had his schedule been clear he would have been happy to appear in Doctor Who.

(374) Jodie Whittaker was nearly cast in a supporting role for one of the episodes in Matt Smith's first season as the Doctor.

(375) Bernard Cribbins was actually considered for the part of the Fourth Doctor.

(376) Michael Hordern, distinguished star of the stage and screen and voice of Paddington bear, was considered to play the Second Doctor.

(377) Peter Capaldi has said he has no great interest in coming back for a 'multi Doctor' episode because he doesn't think they work very well.

(378) A large number of actors have appeared in both Game of Thrones and Doctor Who. Maisie Williams, David Bradley, Joe Dempsie, Lucian Msamati, Harry Lloyd, Mark Gatiss, Paul Kaye and many others.

(379) After the sad death of Elisabeth Sladen, Elisabeth's daughter Sadie Miller took over playing Sarah Jane Smith in the Big Finish audio stories.

(380) Russell T Davies said he has no problem with rewriting Doctor Who canon or changing the show's history.

(381) Chris Chibnall said he was determined to cast a female Doctor when he became showrunner and he was true to his word.

(382) Tom Baker was in 172 episodes. He also appeared in Day of the Doctor.

(383) An asteroid discovered in 1984 was given the name TARDIS in tribute to Doctor Who.

(384) Sherlock Holmes was an influence on the character of the Doctor.

(385) The Doctor has a strong aversion to guns and prefers to outwit his enemies rather than resorting to violence.

(386) The first time we see the Eleventh Doctor after Ten has regenerated, he spits on the TARDIS console. Matt Smith did this on instinct because he had dust in his mouth but they decided to keep it in the episode.

(387) The Judoon are a rhinoceros-headed humanoid species known for their strict, militaristic behavior and their enforcement of the law across the galaxy. The Judoon are often hired as intergalactic police officers or mercenaries to track down fugitives and enforce justice. They are recognised by their distinctive black armour and blaster weapons.

(388) Steven Moffat got the idea for Blink from a spooky angel statue he saw in a graveyard.

(389) Andrew Garfield was in Daleks in Manhattan. Garfield would go on to (among other things) play Spider-Man.

(390) David Tennant and Catherine Tate became good friends through Doctor Who. This is very apparent in the chemistry between the Doctor and Donna.

(391) The Thijarians in Demons of the Punjab have a vague Cenobite/Hellraiser sort of look which is quite good fun.

(392) Peter Kay said he was disappointed by the episode Love & Monsters when he watched it. He was not alone!

(393) Far too much money was spent on The End of the World - the second episode of the relaunched Doctor Who in 2005. As a consequence of this money was very tight for the rest of the first series.

(394) Tom Baker would sometimes make personal appearances in his Doctor Who costume.

(395) Noel Clarke, who played Mickey Smith in the new post 2005 Doctor Who, was no stranger to rebooting old shows because at the time he had recently appeared in the BBC's successful revival of the classic 80s ITV show Auf Wiedersehen, Pet.

(396) When the show came back in 2005, the first episode Rose leaked on internet torrents a month before it was broadcast. The leaked episode differed from the broadcast version because Murray Gold's score wasn't in place.

(397) Tim Curry was a popular choice to play the Doctor in the 1996 television movie but this obviously didn't transpire in the end.

(398) The Two Doctors has a less than hidden subtext about the evils of eating meat. The writer Robert Holmes was a vegetarian.

(399) Eve of the Daleks was the first of the three specials which marked the end of the Jodi/Chibnall era. It was broadcast on New Year's Day in 2022. After the events of the Flux, the Doctor, Yaz, and Dan find themselves in a storage warehouse in Manchester run by a woman named Sarah (Aisling Bea). Sarah is visited by a man named Nick (Adjani Salmon) who has a crush on her. A Dalek appears and wreaks havoc but the TARDIS resetting itself creates a repeating time loop. This creates a Groundhog Day situation where the Doctor and the other characters must find a way to defeat the Dalek. There is a twist though because with each loop the time shortens - leaving them less time to carry out a successful plan.

Eve of the Daleks is hardly original (we've seen a time loop plot like this in countless episodes of Star Trek let alone other science fiction and fantasy shows) and it feels a bit tiresome for Chibnall to (ahem) wheel the Daleks out YET again for a special but this is an episode that works reasonably well and holds up to a repeat viewing a lot better than most of the Chibnall era Who stuff.

(400) Chris Chibnall knew Jodie Whittaker very well before Doctor Who because they had worked on Broadchurch together.

(401) Shane Richie said he was approached about playing the

Doctor when the show came back but he couldn't pursue this because he had signed a contract with EastEnders.

(402) When the show came back in 2005, Edgar Wright turned down an offer to direct the first new Doctor Who episode because he was too busy making Shaun of the Dead.

(403) Russell T Davies said that when the BBC first began to think about bringing Doctor Who back in the early 2000s they actually wanted Tom Baker to play the part again. Russell didn't think this was a very good idea.

(404) Rose Tyler lives in a Peckham tower block. This was seen by many as a little nod to Only Fools and Horses.

(405) Sylvester McCoy's era was panned at the time but seems to have a better reputation today.

(406) Older fans of Classic Who can sometimes be a bit sniffy about NuWho - especially the Chris Chibnall era and the second RTD era.

(407) Billie Piper had three number one hits in Britain during her teenage singing career.

(408) Despite its poor reputation, Love & Monsters actually got quite good reviews from critics when it came out.

(409) Fear Her is generally considered to be the weakest episode of the David Tennant era. This episode suffered from budget cuts and a very short shooting schedule - all of which is evident in the finished product.

(410) Runaway Bride was supposed to have a sequence at Stonehenge but this never happened in the end.

(411) Steven Moffat was apparently happy for David Tennant to continue as the Doctor when he took over as showrunner but David decided to bow out with Russell T Davies.

(412) Jon Pertwee said he had three nice lunches with the BBC before agreeing to play the Doctor!

(413) Brian Blessed said he was approached to play the Second Doctor but declined the role to take another job. He later appeared as King Yrcanos in The Trial of a Time Lord.

(414) Sophie Aldred did a lot of her own stunts as Ace in Doctor Who.

(415) The Haunting of Villa Diodati, which is one of the better episodes of the Chibnall era, has the Doctor meeting Mary Shelley. Frankenstein was written by Mary Shelley when she was only eighteen years-old. Frankenstein is a pioneering work of science fiction and an enduring touchstone of horror. To this day, rarely a year goes past without a film that was inspired by Frankenstein going into production. It is hard to think of any work of fiction that has been as influential as Frankenstein was to the horror genre. The book was written in 1818 while Mary was staying a villa near Geneva close to Lord Byron. The story was, appropriately enough, inspired by a nightmare.

The story in Frankenstein is told through the letters of an explorer named Captain Robert Walton. Walton is on an exploration of the North Pole and runs into a mysterious and cultivated Swiss scientist named Victor Frankenstein. Frankenstein has discovered a way to bring life to body parts that were previously dead. He has meddled with things that shouldn't really have been meddled with at all. The end result is the creation of a monster who inspires fear but only wants to be loved and accepted. We are faced with the realisation that the real monster may not be this unfortunate creature but Victor Frankenstein himself.

(416) Elisabeth Sladen said the TARDIS interior was so cheap during her time on the show that bits of the set sometimes used to fall off during a scene.

(417) Sylvester McCoy was cast as the Doctor because John Nathan Turner wanted more humour in the show after criticism from Michael Grade that it had become too dark and violent. McCoy's Doctor did become quite dark in the end though.

(418) The Doctor has a unique ability to detect disturbances in the fabric of time and space, allowing him to sense when something is amiss.

(419) King Charles has been a fan of Doctor Who since he was a teenager.

(420) Amicus were more interested in making a Doctor Who film that might appeal to kids rather than making a film that might impress Terry Nation. While this meant the film would have limited appeal for Doctor Who purists going forward, it was a sensible business decision at time because Dr Who and the Daleks was one of the top twenty films at the British box-office in 1965.

(421) There is a scene in the first season with Matt Smith where Amy Pond tries to seduce the Doctor. Many fans felt this scene was out of place in Doctor Who. Steven Moffat later seemed to admit it was a mistake.

(422) The unmistakable TARDIS sound effect was originally

created by stroking the bass strings of a piano with a key.

(423) Colin Baker's Doctor was criticised for being too bombastic and aggressive when he took over. Colin said the idea was that we would gradually see him transform into the kind gentle Doctor we know and love. Alas though he never actually got the time to do this.

(424) Vincent Price expressed interest in playing the villain in the aborted Doctor Who Meets Scratchman film that Tom Baker tried to make.

(425) Sergei Subotsky, son of the Amicus producer Milton Subotsky, said that the concept for the third Amicus Doctor Who film (which obviously never got made in the end) was going to be Cushing's Doctor having to work with a younger version of himself to battle crab monsters!

(426) Steven Moffat wanted Matt Smith's Doctor have a pirate themed costume but Matt wanted to wear a bow tie and jacket like a professor.

(427) Bill Nighy told the Daily Express that he turned down the part of the Doctor in the NuWho era because the part came with too much baggage.

(428) Before she was cast as Amy Pond, Karen Gillan had a small part in Fires of Pompeii - an episode which also featured Peter Capaldi.

(429) Hugh David was the first choice of producer Rex Tucker to be the first Doctor but the incoming producer Verity Lambert felt David was too young. Hugh David, for his part, said he wasn't keen on the role because he didn't relish the prospect of fame very much. He later became a television

director.

(430) Peter Capaldi decided not to stay with the show when Chris Chibnall took over. He wanted to bow out with Steven Moffat.

(431) There were plans for Sylvester McCoy's Doctor to be revealed as a powerful big cheese from Gallifrey's history but the show was axed before any of this could be done.

(432) It was never really explained who exactly Tom Baker's 'curator' in Day of the Doctor really was. It is up to fans to come up with their own theory.

(433) At the time of its release, Day of the Doctor was the largest ever simulcast of a TV drama.

(434) Although it sounds insane today, the BBC in the 1960s would often tape over the tape of an episode that had been transmitted - thus erasing that episode. It obviously never occurred to them that people in the future might enjoy watching old television shows. There are still many missing episodes of Doctor Who but the hope is that some of them might turn up one day.

(435) The two part finale to Peter Capaldi's first season copped some criticism for being too dark with its implications that the dead feel pain.

(436) Paul McGann said that, in his opinion, the Doctor Who television film wasn't quite good enough to be deserving of a series.

(437) The two-part finale to the 2024 series was shown in some British cinemas. Many who made the trip to the cinema

were rather disappointed though by the anti-climatic nature of Empire of Death.

(438) NuWho introduced psychic paper. When people look at the Doctor's psychic paper they see whatever they WANT to see. The Doctor often uses it to create fake ID.

(439) The closing credits for the episode Rosa eschew the Doctor Who theme in favour of "Rise Up" by Andra Day.

(440) Comedian, actor, and former Goon Show star Michael Bentine was approached to play the Fourth Doctor but nothing came of it. Bentine is alleged to have wanted too much creative control over how he would play the part.

(441) The Doctor has two hearts.

(442) Frazier Hines said he never had a single disagreement or cross word with Patrick Troughton during their time together on Doctor Who. He said they got on great and had lots of fun.

(443) The 1996 Doctor Who movie was a BBC/Universal co-production and filmed in Canada.

(444) The Woman Who Fell to Earth, the first episode with Jodie Whittaker, got an incredible 10.96 million viewers in Britain. Alas though, the show couldn't manage to hold its audience. The penultimate special with Jodi, Legend of the Sea Devils, only got 3.47 million.

(445) The Tom Baker era story The Sontaran Experiment did some location shooting on Dartmoor.

(446) Tom Baker was working on a building site when he was hired to play the Doctor because his acting jobs were not quite

paying the bills at the time.

(447) Billie Piper asked for Rose to be a bit funnier in season two of NuWho because she felt she'd had a lot of emotional material in the first season and wanted a few lighter scenes.

(448) The big reveal at the end of the first Spyfall episode is that the Master is back (and played with enjoyable glee and gusto by Sacha Dhawan). It is not explained though how we went from Missy (who perished at the end of Capaldi's run) to Sacha Dhawan's Master.

(449) Dad's Army star John Le Mesurier was considered for the part of the Third Doctor but he had no interest in the role because he didn't want to commit himself to another television show.

(450) Eric Roberts, who played the Master in the 1996 television film, is the brother of Hollywood star Julia Roberts.

(451) There was a lot of speculation that Matt Smith and Peter Capaldi were going to be in the 2023 anniversary specials but this obviously didn't happen in the end.

(452) Maisie Williams said she would happily come back to Doctor Who to play Ashildr again.

(453) The actor and singer Tommy Steele was seriously considered as a replacement for William Hartnell when the show had to recast its lead for the first time.

(454) Ben Daniels was seriously considered for the Twelfth Doctor but pipped at the post by Peter Capaldi.

(455) Neil Patrick Harris said he didn't know much about

Doctor Who when he agreed to play The Toymaster in The Giggle. He took the job because he had worked with Russell T Davies on the acclaimed Channel 4 show It's a Sin.

(456) It was Tom Baker's role in The Golden Voyage of Sinbad that made the powers that be think he might be a great Doctor.

(457) The cloak worn by the Third Doctor was apparently something that Jon Pertwee found in his attic.

(458) Twice Upon a Time was basically a bonus Peter Capaldi episode that Steven Moffat produced because Chris Chibnall said he wouldn't have enough time to do a Christmas episode with his new Doctor.

(459) Patrick Troughton died while he was in the United States to attend a science fiction convention.

(460) The episode title Spyfall is obviously a riff on the Bond film Skyfall.

(461) Russell T Davies told the media that he was brought back for a second stint as showrunner with a brief to bring in younger viewers. Though he claimed to be successful in that aim there is scant evidence from the viewing figures to back up that claim.

(462) Eric Saward, the script editor circa John Nathan Turner, was later pretty open about the fact that he didn't agree with Colin Baker being cast as the Doctor.

(463) Matthew Horne was considered for the Eleventh Doctor. Horne is best known for the comedy drama Gavin & Stacey.

(464) John Nathan Turner didn't live long enough to see Doctor Who come back. He died in 2002 at the age of 54. Years of heavy drinking are believed to have been a big factor in his declining health and early death.

(465) The slide in viewing figures for NuWho began in the Peter Capaldi era so it's not a new phenomenon.

(466) Tom Baker broke his collarbone shooting The Sontaran Experiment so they had to use doubles for a number of scenes.

(467) Russell T Davies once called Colin Baker's Doctor Who costume the 'greatest mistake in the history of television'.

(468) The show's iconic theme music was composed by Ron Grainer and realised by Delia Derbyshire at the BBC Radiophonic Workshop.

(469) When the show was in limbo in the 1990s there were periodically press stories about how the show might be resurrected as a film or American series with highly improbable names like Bill Cosby, Michael Jackson, and Jim Carrey lined up to play the Doctor. These stories were taken with a tanker truck of salt.

(470) The Fifteenth Doctor's sonic looks a bit like a television remote control. Russell T Davies said he felt the old sonic looked too much like a gun.

(471) Jon Pertwee said that Roger Delgado was a lovely and kind man in real life and nothing at all like the Master.

(472) Had he returned as boss in 1987, co-creator Sydney Newman proposed that Patrick Troughton should come back for a season and then regenerate into a female Doctor.

(473) Rose was the first Doctor Who episode to be named after a companion.

(474) John Nathan Turner once said 'there will be no hanky panky in the TARDIS' during his tenure. He was strict about the Doctor being an asexual and somewhat aloof character who has no romantic or lustful feelings towards his companions or people he meets.

(475) Frazier Hines was only supposed to be in one episode as Jamie McCrimmon but they liked the character so much they made him a regular.

(476) Tom Hanks is said to be a big Doctor Who fan.

(477) Doctor Who is the world's longest running sci-fi show.

(478) City of Death, with the Fourth Doctor, got an incredible 16 million viewers in Britain.

(479) The Eleventh Doctor created a boost for sales of bow-ties in clothing stores.

(480) Tom Baker displayed a great gift for comedy in his career after Doctor Who. He gave a memorable performance in Blackadder II and was also the narrator for the sketch comedy series Little Britain.

(481) The Weeping Angels are known for their ability to feed off the potential time energy of their victims, sending them back in time to live out their lives in the past. They appear as statues when observed, but can move quickly and attack when not being looked at.

(482) It is believed that, after David Tennant left, Chiwetel

Ejiofor was offered the part of the Doctor by Steven Moffat but was not available.

(483) World's End is a 1964 Doctor Who episode directed by Richard Martin. This begins The Dalek Invasion of Earth arc - a story that was later recycled for the Peter Cushing Amicus Who films. This is a fantastically creepy episode that finds the TARDIS landing in the London of the future but finding only ruins and plague, mankind in tatters. It appears those hardy villains the Daleks have been up to mischief again, this time an invasion of Earth.

The black and white lends these early Doctor Who adventures a grainy and strange atmosphere that works very well in the intimacy of television. The special effects are rather dated of course and the budgets clearly not exactly lavish but William Hartnell makes for a fine interpretation of the Doctor. It's especially interesting to note how low-key this is played at times by the actors. If anything this approach adds to the weird atmosphere and makes the quiet reflective moments all the more effective.

(484) Robert Holmes was not a huge fan of the Daleks.

(485) Leslie Grantham appeared in two episodes of Resurrection of the Daleks. This was a year before he became famous for playing 'Dirty' Den Watts in the soap opera EastEnders.

(486) Colin Baker said The Ultimate Foe was his favourite story out of the ones he appeared in.

(487) Bernard Cribbins, by now in his 90s, returned as Wilf for the 2023 anniversary specials but sadly could only film one scene (the end of Wild Blue Yonder). He passed away not long

afterwards.

(488) Dr Who and the Daleks is no masterpiece but it's a lively and well made children's film with some amusing moments and fun production design. It's the sort of thing you'd watch half-asleep on a Sunday afternoon and perfectly passable if one's expectations aren't unduly high.

(489) The Doctor has a deep knowledge of science and technology, often using his intellect to solve complex problems and overcome seemingly impossible challenges.

(490) The Doctor's sonic screwdriver is capable of opening locks, scanning for information, and disabling electronic devices.

(491) The peak popularity of NuWho was the first RTD era during David Tennant's run. Though the conditions were more favourable back then in that more people still watched traditional television than they do today, it is still fair to say that Tennant was by far the most popular Doctor of the NuWho era and the show has plainly struggled ever since to find a lead actor who can match that appeal to casual audiences.

(492) Steven Moffat said he wasn't a big fan of The Beast Below - which was the second episode he did with Matt Smith.

(493) David Jason was courted for the part of Mr Copper in Voyage of the Damned but he wasn't available.

(494) Time Crash is a mini-episode broadcast as part of the BBC's Children in Need appeal in 2007. It features the Tenth Doctor meeting his fifth incarnation in a time crash caused by the TARDISes of both Doctors being in close proximity to each

other.

(495) Charlie Brooker said he was once asked to write an episode of Doctor Who but couldn't do it because he didn't have the time. Brooker created the anthology series Black Mirror.

(496) The Toymaker was originally played by Michael Gough. Neil Patrick Harris took over the part when the character returned in 2023.

(497) Richard Ayoade, the comic actor and television presenter, is a name that is frequently thrown up by fans and bookies lists when it comes to casting the Doctor. He certainly had the eccentricity to be the Doctor but his weakness was his acting ability. Ayoade is funny and eccentric but he is no actor.

(498) Billie Piper said that Father's Day was her favourite episode out of the ones she appeared in.

(499) Colin Baker said The Two Doctors was one of his favourite episodes because he got to work with Patrick Troughton.

(500) Chris Chibnall's Timeless Child arc begs a number of pedantic questions. How come Clara didn't see any of these other gazillions of Doctors when she entered Matt Smith's timestream? Why has the Fugitive Doctor got a police box TARDIS?

(501) Peter Cushing was apparently not in the best of health when Invasion Earth 2150 A.D. was made and was absent for early shooting so the supporting characters get more screen time than they might have done otherwise. We got a lot more

of the slapstick antics of Bernard Cribbins than was originally planned as a consequence.

(502) Steven Moffat was always the obvious choice to replace Russell T Davies as showrunner because he was clearly the stand-out guest writer during the first Davies era. During the time that Davies was in charge of Doctor Who, Moffat wrote episodes like The Girl in the Fireplace, Blink, Silence in the Library, and The Empty Child.

(503) After the departure of Peter Capaldi, one of the favourites with the bookies was Kris Marshall - the speculation only increased by his sudden decision to leave the popular BBC show Death in Paradise. Marshall played an eccentric detective in the show and was known for comic roles in the past. This all made him seem like someone who might be a good fit for the part of the Doctor. Fans didn't seem very impressed by the prospect of Marshall playing the Doctor though. His casting seemed too obvious and safe. As it turned out he wasn't even in contention at all.

(504) The APC in James Cameron's Aliens patently inspired the vehicle in Orphan 55.

(505) The Thirteenth Doctor met Ada Lovelace. Ada Lovelace was a pioneer in early computers.

(506) The part of the Master was created and written by Barry Letts specifically for Roger Delgado.

(507) The TARDIS interior in series eleven looks ridiculous when the characters are all there. It's so small they have nowhere to stand. It just looks like a small empty room with a couple of plastic props that are supposed to be crystals.

(508) Ursula is turned into a paving slab at the end of Love &
Monsters but Elton implies they still maintain a relationship.
This was a rather bizarre and risque joke by Russell T Davies.

(509) Matt Smith said he had to do two secret auditions before
he was cast as the Doctor.

(510) Steven Moffat said that being in charge of Doctor Who is
a difficult job because you have to come up with a new
interesting standalone plot for each episode. You can't make a
season of Doctor Who like a long movie because it is generally
episodic in nature.

(511) It is noticeable that when Thirteen regenerates into
Fourteen, they chose not to have David Tennant wear Jodie's
costume. Fourteen regenerates right into his new clothes!

(512) The Fifth Doctor wore a piece of celery on his lapel as a
prevention against Praxis Range gas. If the celery turned
purple he would eat it and this would save him.

(513) John Hurt was the first person to play the Doctor with a
beard.

(514) Fawlty Towers star Andrew Sachs was considered for the
part of the Seventh Doctor. He later voiced Adric in the Big
Finish story The Boy That Time Forgot.

(515) John Hurt didn't have to audition for Day of the Doctor.
He was simply offered the part and accepted.

(516) Nichola Bryant said Timelash was her least favourite
story. She didn't much enjoy Peri being tied up.

(517) Over ten million people watched the first episode Rose

when the show returned in 2005.

(518) Peter Capaldi's Doctor had a beautiful red velvet lined black jacket in his first season. However, his costume seemed to change a lot later on.

(519) Steven Moffat said it was incredibly 'depressing' when he couldn't persuade Christopher Eccleston to do The Day of the Doctor because Eccleston's Doctor played a big part in his original version of the script.

(520) Jon Pertwee's departure from Doctor Who was not just because of other cast members leaving and the tragic death of Roger Delgado but also because he was frustrated by the BBC's refusal to give him a pay increase. Pertwee also suffered from back problems so was struggling with the workload of the show.

(521) Long before Doctor Who came along, Christopher Eccleston and David Tennant were both in the 1996 film Jude.

(522) Jon Pertwee's era was the most UNIT focused the show has ever been.

(523) David Tennant said it was a great wrench to leave Doctor Who the first time around but he thought it was best to leave people wanting more rather than stay on for too long and potentially overstay your welcome.

(524) The Ninth Doctor's catchphrase was "Fantastic!"

(525) Jodie Whittaker said that David Tennant was her favourite Doctor. Jodie and David both worked together on Broadchurch.

(526) One of the reasons for Doctor Who being away from television for so long post 1989 is that the BBC were hopeful that someone might make a Doctor Who feature film. This obviously never happened though.

(527) Chris Chibnall's first season as showrunner eschewed Doctor Who's classic monsters like Daleks and Cybermen. He brought them back later on though.

(528) The return of Russell T Davies as showrunner saw a new partnership deal between the BBC and Disney to help fund the show. One might argue though that increased funding for the show hasn't been blindingly obvious onscreen as the show doesn't look that much better than it did in the Chibnall era.

(529) When he became showrunner, Steven Moffat is alleged to have strongly considered Paterson Joseph to play the Doctor. Paterson, had he been cast back then, would have been the first black actor to play the Doctor.

(530) The participation of Disney in the second RTD era has sadly been a red flag to a bull for conservative YouTube grifters - who now spend much of their time making clickbait videos trashing the show.

(531) Despite being the youngest Doctor when he was cast, Matt Smith drew praise for the way he managed to convey an old soul in a young body.

(532) One of the problems that modern Doctor Who faces is the preposterous amount of content out there vying for our attention in this frenzied streaming age. Shows like The Expanse do serious sci-fi and shows like Fallout do offbeat sci-fi. Doctor Who now has more competition than ever in the field it helped pioneer.

(533) Ben Whishaw was a popular suggestion to play the Doctor in the last few castings but he's an actor who is probably too 'big' for Doctor Who now. Whishaw was an unrealistic suggestion from the get go.

(534) Doctor Who and the Mines of Terror is a 1985 computer game which appeared on the BBC Micro, Amstrad CPC and Commodore 64. The game is a platform arcade adventure. The C64 version got a very respectable 86% in the famous magazine Zzap!64. The Doctor in the game is Colin Baker.

(535) Russell T Davies said that Ruby Sunday's arc was inspired by Rey in the Star Wars films. Russell said he liked the idea that Rey was just an ordinary person - before this was changed.

(536) Dalek Attack is a 1992 computer game which appeared on various systems - including MS-DOS, the Amiga and C64. This is considered to be one of the best Doctor Who games. It has crisp polished graphics and is a side-scrolling action adventure in which you choose from a range of Doctors to control.

(537) Doctor Who and the Warlord is a 1985 text adventure for the BBC Micro. It was supposed to get a Spectrum release but this never happened. It is probably fair to say this game is a bit forgotten now.

(538) Peter Purves played a number of roles in Doctor Who before essaying the part of companion Steven Taylor. Purves would become best known as a presenter - most notably for Blue Peter.

(539) Doctor Who: Destiny of the Doctors is a 1997 game for Microsoft Windows. This is a first person game which takes

place mostly in the TARDIS. Tom Baker, Peter Davison, Colin Baker, Sylvester McCoy and Nicholas Courtney lent their voices to the game and there is archive audio of Who actors who had passed away. Destiny of the Doctors got middling reviews. What killed the game more than anything is that it was released around the same time as Quake II.

(540) Anthony Ainley was the fourth actor to play the Master and appeared in 31 episodes as this famous villain. All of Ainley's appearances came in the 1980s.

(541) Peter Pratt played the Master in the 1976 story The Deadly Assassin. He had big shoes to fill after the death of Roger Delgado but did a very creditable job.

(542) The director David Yates, best known for Harry Potter, told the media in 2011 that he was working on a Doctor Who feature film that would be separate from the television show. Nothing came of this in the end and Steven Moffat (who was in charge of the television show at the time) later denied that it had even been close to being made.

(543) Billie Piper said that when she came back in 2008 she struggled to remember how to do Rose Tyler's voice again because she doesn't speak like Rose in real life.

(544) When they made The Three Doctors, Jon Pertwee said he was a bit irritated by Patrick Troughton's habit of ad libbing and throwing in slightly eccentric line deliveries. The two men did become good friends though.

(545) William Hartnell's wife said he was never happier than during his time on Doctor Who. He truly loved playing the character.

(546) The Impossible Astronaut is dedicated to Elisabeth Sladen.

(547) Patrick Troughton's Doctor can be seen in a panel of Alan Moore's The League Of Extraordinary Gentlemen Century 1969.

(548) Steven Moffat said that The Big Bang was one of his favourite episodes out of the ones he wrote for Doctor Who.

(549) The William Hartnell and Matt Smith incarnations of the Doctor both appear very briefly in Alan Moore's The League Of Extraordinary Gentlemen Century 2009. The two Doctors look directly at us as if they know what is going on but have decided they can't interfere.

(550) David Walliams was apparently a candidate to be the Tenth Doctor. It is difficult to imagine he would have had the gravitas for the part.

(551) Cardiff doubled for New York and Area 51 in Day of the Moon.

(552) In the episode The Devil's Chord, the Doctor meets The Beatles. We don't hear any Beatles music at all though in the episode.

(553) Captain Jack was supposed to appear in A Good Man Goes to War but John Barrowman couldn't do it because he was too busy filming Torchwood.

(554) Jemma Redgrave as made her first appearance as Kate Stewart in the Matt Smith era episode The Power of Three.

(555) Christopher Eccleston's first director on Doctor Who was

Keith Boak. By all accounts these two men did not get on at all. Eccleston was unhappy at the way Boak treated extras and also staged dangerous sequences without seeming to have the expertise to do so safely. A lot of Boak's footage was deemed unusable. Eccleston said that if Joe Aherne had directed the first block of episodes in 2005 then he wouldn't have soured on the show so quickly and wouldn't have left.

(556) John Barrowman was openly critical of Steven Moffat and blamed Moffat for Captain Jack not making any appearances during the Smith and Capaldi eras. It was Chris Chibnall who finally brought Captain Jack back.

(557) Steven Berkoff was allegedly rather difficult to work with on The Power of Three.

(558) John Barrowman had to dye his hair to play Captain Jack in the Chibnall era because he'd gone grey in real life.

(559) The Doctor is able to visit any point in time and space, from historical events to alien planets.

(560) Tom Baker was not a big fan of John Nathan Turner. He left the show just as the JNT era was beginning.

(561) Jodie Whittaker's Doctor was depicted as a somewhat androgynous character. They pointedly never put Jodie in a dress or feminine clothes - even in period episodes.

(562) Neil Gaiman was openly critical of Steven Moffat for tinkering with his Nightmare In Silver script and making it worse. Though he didn't mention Moffat by name, Steven Moffat was obviously the only person who had the power to edit the scripts.

(563) The TARDIS stands for Time And Relative Dimension In Space.

(564) Matt Smith was apparently paid £200,000 a year when he became the Doctor.

(565) Andrew Keir, who would play Professor Bernard Quatermass in Hammer's classic 1967 film Quatermass and the Pit, is also in the cast of Daleks' Invasion Earth 2150 A.D. as Wyler.

(566) The Doctor's TARDIS was originally going to change into a different object each week to blend into its surroundings. This was changed in order to keep the budget down. The explanation in the show is that the chameleon circuit broke and so the TARDIS is now stuck as a 1963 police box.

(567) Peter Davison said that Patrick Troughton advised him not to do Doctor Who for longer than three years.

(568) Hammer horror icon Ingrid Pitt was the guest star in Warriors of the Deep. Pitt was also in The Time Monster with Jon Pertwee.

(569) Steven Moffat said he was hurt at times by the fan criticism he got during his time in charge of Doctor Who.

(570) Peter Capaldi was in the Tennant episode The Fires Of Pompeii and also Torchwood before he was cast as the Doctor. We see in Capaldi's Doctor Who run that The Fires Of Pompeii inspired the face he chose. We never got an explanation though for why his Doctor looked like a Torchwood character.

(571) Peter Cushing said he enjoyed playing Doctor Who because it was nice to take a break from horror roles and do

something that children could watch. "Those films are among my favourites because they brought me popularity with younger children. They'd say their parents didn't want to meet me in a dark alley but Doctor Who changed that. After all, he is one of the most heroic and successful parts an actor can play. That's one of the main reasons the series had such a long run on TV. I am very grateful for having been part of such a success story."

(572) You may recognise Philip Madoc, who plays Brockley, in the film Daleks' Invasion Earth 2150 A.D. Madoc played the German U-boat captain in the "Don't tell him Pike!" episode of Dad's Army.

(573) Jodie Whittaker did a lot of her own stunts in The Woman Who Fell to Earth.

(574) Tom Baker would sometimes talk over the other actors during a scene. This is because he hadn't read other parts of the script and was generally doing his own thing anyway. This does though give his Doctor a charismatic authority. He commandingly takes charge of the situation in a way that some of the later NuWho actors struggled to do.

(575) Matthew Waterhouse, who played Adric, said he found it much easier to work with Peter Davison than he did Tom Baker.

(576) Cheryl Hall and Jenny McCracken were both considered for the part of Jo Grant.

(577) As a young man, Tom Baker spent several years as a monk in Jersey. He said he gave it up after losing his faith.

(578) The Chris Chibnall era has an episode which revolves

around Rosa Parks. Rosa Parks was born Rosa Louise McCauley in Tuskegee, Alabama, on February 4, 1913. She became active in the civil rights struggle as far back as the 1940s - her husband was a member of The National Association for the Advancement of Colored People (NAACP). She worked for the local NAACP leader Edgar Nixon and Parks and her husband were members of the League of Women Voters. In Montgomery, Alabama, on December 1, 1955, Parks refused to obey bus driver James F. Blake's order that she give up her seat in the "colored" section to a white passenger. Because of her defiance the Montgomery Bus Boycott became an important and enduring symbol of the Civil Rights movement.

"I had given up my seat before, but this day, I was especially tired," said Rosa. "Tired from my work as a seamstress, and tired from the ache in my heart. As far back as I can remember, I knew there was something wrong with our way of life when people could be mistreated because of the color of their skin." In the 1960s Rosa Parks worked for John Conyers (who served as a U.S. Representative for Michigan from 1965 to 2017) and befriended Malcolm X. She was involved in activism and campaigned to reverse the lack of housing for black people in Detroit.

Rosa Parks later founded the Detroit chapter of the Joann Little Defense Committee and co-founded the Rosa L. Parks Scholarship Foundation for college-bound high school seniors. She was widowed in the 1980s and because she was prone to donating her speaking fees to charitable causes, Rosa never had much money. She was sometimes too generous for her own good. Rosa Parks died of natural causes on October 24, 2005, at the age of 92, in her apartment on the east side of Detroit. When the apartment she had lived in was threatened with demolition an artist had it rebuilt in Germany as a Rosa Parks museum. When Rosa died, her body was transported to

Washington, D.C. and transported by a bus similar to the one in which she made her protest, to lie in honour in the rotunda of the U.S. Capitol. Since the founding of the practice in 1852, Parks was the 31st person, the first American who had not been a U.S. government official, and the second private person to be honoured in this way. She was the first woman and the second black person to lie in honour in the Capitol.

Asked how she wanted to be remembered, Rosa Parks said - "I would like to be remembered as a person who wanted to be free so other people would be also free." Her defiance during the civil rights struggle and participation in activism has secured Rosa Parks a lasting legacy in history

(579) The TARDIS is alive in a sense, with its own consciousness and ability to communicate with the Doctor.

(580) One fan complaint about Ncuti Gatwa's Fifteenth Doctor is that he doesn't seem to have a costume and wears completely different clothes from week to week. This is obviously a deliberate choice by Russell T Davies but it does make the character feel more generic when you just put him in a leather jacket or orange jumper.

(581) The Thirteenth Doctor met Nikola Tesla. Nikola Tesla was a Serbian-American inventor, electrical engineer, mechanical engineer, and physicist. He is best known for his contributions to the design of the modern alternating current (AC) electricity supply system. Tesla also invented many other technologies and had over 300 patents in his name. He was a pioneer in the development of radio and wireless communication, as well as X-ray technology.

(582) Matt Smith's contract with the BBC expired just before The Name of the Doctor so they had to agree a new short term

contract with him.

(583) John Hurt turned down the part of the War Doctor initially but was persuaded to take the role by his wife.

(584) In the two part finale to the 2024 series, Russell T Davies revealed that Sutekh has been clinging to the TARDIS for all these years and has finally revealed himself. The contradictions this created led fans to create all sorts of comical memes.

(585) Sylvester McCoy said he was slightly disappointed that he wasn't asked to participate in The Day of the Doctor. Sylvester did appear through archive footage though.

(586) Gareth Roberts was a writer on Doctor Who from 2005 to 2014 and also worked on the The Sarah Jane Adventures and wrote some Doctor Who novels. Roberts is alleged to have had a blazing row with Peter Capaldi during the production of the episode The Caretaker and then later took to Twitter to slag off Steven Moffat (before deleting the tweets). Roberts also (unwisely perhaps) waded into the dreaded culture wars and made some comments about how (in his view) it was impossible for someone to change their biological sex. Needless to say, Gareth Roberts had no further involvement in Doctor Who.

(587) The actor, presenter, and comedian Alan Davies was often cited as one of the frontrunners to play the Doctor when the show came back under Russell T Davies. However, despite all the press Alan Davies said he was never approached about the role and it was all media speculation.

(588) Philip Madoc was not just in Daleks' Invasion Earth: 2150 A.D. He was also in the television show - specifically The

Krotons, The War Games, The Brain of Morbius, and The Power of Kroll.

(589) Peter Davison's hair was made lighter when he played the Doctor because they wanted him to be a contrast to his illustrious predecessor Tom Baker.

(590) The Eleventh Doctor was known for his love of fish fingers and custard.

(591) Olivia Colman was often cited by the media and fans when it came to finding the Thirteenth Doctor but this was always an unlikely prospect because Colman was picking up film roles and unlikely to want to be tied down to a television show.

(592) The Doctor has a great fondness for Earth and its inhabitants.

(593) Colin Baker famously hated his garish Doctor costume. The showrunner John Nathan Turner was fond of Hawaiian shirts and this is what gave him the idea for the costume.

(594) Verity Lambert said Doctor Who was only supposed to run for a year. It obviously lasted a lot longer than that.

(595) David Tennant said that when he was first asked to be the Doctor he was actually hesitant and took a couple of days to agree to do it.

(596) John Nathan Turner had previously worked as a production unit manager on All Creatures Great And Small. It was this show which gave him the idea of casting Peter Davison as the Doctor.

(597) Pip & Jane Baker were a husband and wife writing team known for their work on Doctor Who. They wrote several scripts for the show in the 1980s. Pip and Jane were two of the people that a young Chris Chibnall had a pop at on Open Air. Chris got a taste of his own medicine when his era of Doctor Who copped some brickbats!

(598) Verity Lambert (who obviously had no involvement by this stage) later said she felt the show 'went down the pan' after Peter Davison.

(599) The budget for The Witchfinders episode with the Thirteenth Doctor is so non existent that they don't even have horses. King James has no entourage!

(600) David Tennant said that because NuWho hadn't even come out when he became the Doctor he worried that the show might not get a good reception and put a spanner in the plans of a second season with him replacing Eccleston. Thankfully though it all turned out fine in the end.

(601) Chris Chibnall admitted that The Battle of Ranskoor Av Kolos wasn't very good. He said he ran out of time and couldn't do a second draft of the script.

(602) Richard Griffiths was considered for the part of the Doctor on a couple of occasions in the Classic Who era. He would become best known for the Harry Potter films and his role as Henry Crabbe in Pie In The Sky.

(603) Colin Baker's brief run as the Doctor was not helped by the fact that most kids chose to watch The A-Team on ITV of a Saturday teatime rather than Doctor Who.

(604) Tom Baker holds the record for the longest-serving

actor in the role of the Doctor.

(605) The day before the announcement that Jodie Whittaker was to be the new Doctor there was a frenzied rumour that Daniel Radcliffe had signed to play the role. This rumour naturally turned out to be false.

(606) After the departure of Patrick Troughton, Jon Pertwee's agent wrote to the BBC suggesting him for the part. It turned out though that Jon was already on the shortlist and under consideration.

(607) The Daleks (aka The Dead Planet) is a 1963) episode of Doctor Who where the first Doctor - in the guise of William Hartnell - meets his eternal intergalactic foes the Daleks and people hide behind sofas everywhere as these metal encased baddies enter the pantheon of television history. This arc finds the Doctor trapped on a planet that doesn't quite seem like Earth. Vegetation appears to have died but the nearby city seems to be standing. The Doctor must venture there to look for something and in the process runs into what will become his most obstinate enemy.

This is a fun entry in the long running Doctor Who universe, more talky than more recent converts might be used to and with a special effects budget that would make Blue Peter struggle let alone a science fiction drama. But the story offers some fascinating first details about the titular tin can villains and William Hartnell's more serious grumpy Doctor works very well too in the story. There would be scarier Doctor Who episodes but nothing would quite have the impact of the Daleks meeting us for the first time.

(608) The Fourth Doctor's iconic scarf was the result of a miscommunication between the costume designer and the

knitter, resulting in a much longer scarf than intended.

(609) Before the casting of Peter Capaldi, the Daily Telegraph reported that Rory Kinnear had been chosen to be the new Doctor. Kinnear (best known for playing Tanner in the Bond films) poured cold water on this alleged scoop by saying that he'd never been approached about Doctor Who and had never even seen a single episode of the show.

(610) Roy Castle said he got more letters for appearing in a Doctor Who film than for anything else he ever did.

(611) The sonic screwdriver first appeared in 1968.

(612) A difference between the format of Classic Who and NuWho is that the original show often had half-hour (ish) episodes and a story was spread out over multiple episodes. NuWho is episodic and has hour long episodes - or at least longer episodes.

(613) Some fans felt that the 2024 series with Russell T Davies back at the helm was so underwhelming it actually made the Chibnall era seem better in retrospect!

(614) The 1965 film Dr Who and the Daleks is loosely based on the 1963 television stories The Dead Planet and The Daleks.

(615) Sylvester McCoy was allowed to ad lib a few quips here and there when he played the Doctor.

(616) Billie Piper shot The End of Time in conjunction with appearing in Secret Diary of a Call Girl.

(617) The Eleventh Doctor had a fondness for fezzes.

(618) Peter Davison said one of the reasons he left the show was was he didn't like the Doctor having an American accented companion in Peri (though Nichol Bryant is English in real life). Davision felt this was a cheap gimmick desperately trying to make the show more appealing to Americans.

(619) The end of Orphan 55 is inspired by the end of the original Planet of the Apes film.

(620) Valentine Dyall was approached to play the second Doctor but he wasn't interested. He did though later play the Black Guardian in the show.

(621) The Thirteenth Doctor's companion Ryan Sinclair is dyspraxic (a neurological disorder which affects planning of movements and co-ordination) and so - although he's in his late teens - has not yet mastered the art of riding a bike. Chris Chibnall has a nephew who suffers from dyspraxia so decided to write it into the show through a character to give the condition more publicity.

(622) Nikola Tesla's Night of Terror has a nice subtext about the positive contribution that immigrants can make to a society.

(623) Chris Chibnall never really resolved the cliffhanger of Jodie Whittaker's first appearance when the TARDIS seemed to eject her and she was last seen falling through the sky. What happened afterwards? Well, nothing really. She landed on a train. Are Time Lords invulnerable post-regeneration?

(624) Some fans only like specific eras and some fans like all the eras. It is of course all subjective.

(625) The character/costume theme for Patrick Troughton's Doctor was a 'cosmic hobo'.

(626) The first anniversary special with David Tennant in 2023 had overnight viewing figures of over 5 million. The series which followed next summer with Ncuti Gatwa as the lead saw overnights fall to just over two million. While there are extenuating circumstances (most saliently the episodes streaming on Disney the night before the BBC transmission) the show plainly lost a good chunk of viewers after Tennant's second departure.

(627) The Ood are a peaceful and servile species, known for their telepathic abilities and their distinctive red eyes. Initially portrayed as enslaved by humans and used as servants, the Ood later gain their independence and become more prominent in the series as allies of the Doctor. They are characterised by their tragic history of oppression and their desire for freedom.

(628) Peter Capaldi said that, some years before he replaced Matt Smith as the Doctor, he was asked to audition for the role in the 1996 television film. He declined to do so though because he felt he would have little chance of being cast.

(629) Fulton Mackay was considered for the Fourth Doctor. This was shortly before he landed his most famous role in the sitcom Porridge.

(630) Davros is usually depicted as being in a high tech wheelchair. When the character appeared in the 2023 Children in Need Doctor Who special though he was walking around and didn't have his usual scarred face. Russell T Davies said he made the change because he wasn't comfortable with having a disabled villain. Some fans thought this was a bit

silly.

(631) The Doctor is known for his eccentricities, quick wit, and moral code, which values justice, compassion, and bravery.

(632) Honor Blackman turned down the part of Vivien Fay in The Stones of Blood. It was Susan Engel who played this role in the end.

(633) The dwindling ratings of Doctor Who when it was axed in the 1980s were not helped by the BBC's habit of putting it up against the popular ITV soap opera Coronation Street. Back in those days the soaps used to get huge audiences.

(634) Patrick Troughton and Frazier Hines went on a little strike at one point during the Second Doctor's era because they were fed up being forced to work weekends.

(635) Some feel that Doctor Who has become too preachy during the Chibnall era and second Russell T Davies era - with messages shoehorned in at every opportunity. Doctor Who has never been apolitical though and always had messages about the environment and themes such as fascism and standing up for the oppressed. The problem arises when the themes are not laced organically into an entertaining science fiction story. If an episode is subpar and the themes seem too obvious then the audience will feel as if they are being lectured and patronised. Make the stories great first and then lace in the message. Don't have an obvious patronising message in a dull story. That's the worst of all worlds.

(636) The Fifteenth Doctor defeats Sutekh by putting a dog lead on him (Ruby actually does this) and dragging him through the Time Vortex. It is probably fair to say that some fans thought this was a rather daft and unsatisfying

resolution.

(637) Colin Baker said he was completely befuddled by the story Mindwarp because the producer, script editor, and writer were not getting along and he never got any clear direction or explanation of why the Doctor behaves as he does in the story.

(638) The Doctor's companions often serve as a moral compass, keeping him grounded and reminding him of the importance of empathy and compassion.

(639) Doctor Who fans are known as known as Whovians.

(640) Steven Moffat gave an infamous interview in 1995 where he trashed most of Doctor Who and said he wouldn't advise anyone to watch it. Just about the only aspect of Who he had any praise for was Peter Davison. Moffat has since downplayed the interview and said he was talking nonsense.

(641) In the early 2000s, Mark Gatiss and Gareth Roberts pitched a Doctor Who revival where the Doctor was on Earth as a mysterious gentleman who runs an antiques shop.

(642) Steven Moffat said he didn't love Twice Upon a Time. He thought it could have been better.

(643) Jodie's Thirteenth Doctor wears Peter Capaldi's clothes for most of her first episode. One could argue she seems much more like the Doctor in these clothes than she does in her official outfit!

(644) Steven Moffat said that he knew straight away at the auditions that Matt Smith was going to be the Eleventh Doctor but they only made the official decision two weeks later

because they had to 'second guess' themselves by testing other actors.

(645) Nicola Bryant said that John Nathan Turner told her not to reveal she was married in real life. He obviously felt Peri would be more appealing if she was deemed 'attainable' in real life.

(646) Jodie Whittaker said that she and Chris Chibnall had an agreement where they would do three years of Doctor Who and then leave together.

(647) Patrick Troughton apparently had a lively love life when he played the Doctor because he had a wife and girlfriend he shuttled back and forth between. The wife and girlfriend apparently had no idea each other existed!

(648) Russell T Davies wanted Sophie Aldred to appear as Ace in The Sarah Jane Adventures but sadly this never happened in the end.

(649) During a tense moment in The Time of Angels a graphic appeared on the screen promoting the Graham Norton Show. Doctor Who fans were very annoyed by this and the BBC had to offer an apology. They said there was a mistake and the Graham Norton promo was activated too soon.

(650) The Talons of Weng-Chiang is somewhat problematic in today's climate because it has white actors playing Chinese characters.

(651) Sophie Aldred said she would have happily appeared in the 1996 Doctor Who television film as Ace had she been asked.

(652) Vengeance on Varos has a rather shocking and weird scene where Colin Baker's Doctor pushes two guards into an acid bath. The scene is played for laughs too with jaunty music and a Bond style quip from the Doctor at the end! Needless to say the BBC got a lot of complaints about this.

(653) The Eighth Doctor has a kiss in the 1996 television film - which was something new at the time. Steven Moffat said that Paul McGann's Doctor was an influence on the more romantic versions of the character later played by Tennant and Smith.

(654) Michael Jayston, who played the Valeyard in The Trial Of A Time Lord, was apparently a contender to replace Roger Moore as James Bond in the early 1980s. In the end though Roger signed a new contract.

(655) At the end of The Woman Who Fell to Earth, all of the guest stars in the forthcoming new season are featured in a (slightly pompous) 'coming soon' sort of trailer

(656) Chris Chibnall said the first Doctor Who story he can remember watching as a child was The Sea Devils.

(657) When he was a kid, Peter Capaldi once wrote a letter to the Radio Times praising Doctor Who.

(658) Chris Chibnall somehow kept the casting of the new female Doctor top secret virtually until it was announced. It was a remarkable piece of secrecy. This 'mystery box' would continue as the show entered production. We knew very little about Chibnall's Doctor Who until it actually aired.

(659) Ryan's dyspraxia seems to come and go in series eleven. Sometimes he has it and at other times it's as if Chris Chibnall completely forgot he'd given Ryan this condition in the first

place!

(660) Long before Jodie Whittaker, the BBC toyed (rather tentatively) with the idea of a woman as the Doctor a couple of times in the past but never really went very far with the idea.

(661) Gallifreyan engineering is based on a deep understanding of temporal physics and energy manipulation, allowing the Time Lords to create technologies that are far beyond the capabilities of other civilizations.

(662) The Fourth Doctor was not designed or written in a certain way and so Tom Baker was given freedom to tailor the role to his own taste and personality.

(663) The TARDIS has a perception filter which means that people don't really notice it when it is parked somewhere.

(664) Steven Moffat and Jenna Coleman were both disappointed when Matt Smith decided to move on from Doctor Who though they obviously respected his decision.

(665) In his novelisation of The Day of the Doctor, Steven Moffat has a scene where the two Peter Cushing Dr Who films exist as movies in the Doctor Who universe. The idea of Moffat is that Cushing and the Doctor were friends so the Doctor was happy for Cushing to play him.

(666) Phoebe Waller-Bridge was often mentioned as a candidate to be the first female Doctor when Chibnall took over but this obviously didn't transpire. Waller-Bridge had a Broadchurch link (she was in eight episodes) and was apparently tickled to see her name in the mix but nothing came of this. She was probably too busy for Doctor Who

anyway.

(667) Peter Cushing later played Grand Toff Markin in Star Wars. Cushing said he was somewhat bewildered by his character's name and the script but decided to do the film because he thought it would be something that children in particular would love. His character had to wear tight military style boots but Cushing found they were incredibly painful and uncomfortable and persuaded George Lucas to let him do the rest of his scenes in a pair of slippers!

(668) On November 22, 1987, local viewers in Chicago were shocked when their regularly scheduled programming - which happened to be the Doctor Who episode Horror of Fang Rock - was interrupted by a strange and unsettling figure. The broadcast signal had been hijacked by someone wearing a mask of the character Max Headroom, a computer-generated TV host from a popular show at the time. The hijacker proceeded to taunt and insult the viewers, making crude and nonsensical comments before the signal was abruptly cut off. The incident lasted for just a few minutes, but it caused a sensation and left many people wondering who was behind the bizarre stunt. To this day, the identity of the hijacker remains unknown.

(669) The mist shrouded Antizone in It Takes You Away feels inspired by the Upside Down from Stranger Things.

(670) Yasmin Finney made her debut as Donna Noble's daughter Rose in The Star Beast. Finney was best known for the show Heartstopper.

(671) In the 1960s, a young boy actually won a Dalek as his prize in a Sugar Puffs competition!

(672) The trailers for the launch of the Thirteenth Doctor made use of Macklemore & Skylar Grey's song Glorious.

(673) Terry Nation, up until 1980, lived on the edge of the village Lynsted in Kent. He actually supplied a wooden prop Dalek for the local primary school.

(674) The episode Hide was originally intended to be a Quatermass crossover.

(675) Steven Moffat said he loved the two Amicus films with Peter Cushing as the Doctor.

(676) Kylie Minogue said she was quite nervous doing Doctor Who because she hadn't done much acting for a while.

(677) Peter Cushing said the Daleks got on his nerves a bit when he made the two Amicus films.

(678) Matt Smith had to wear a wig in The Time of the Doctor because he'd shaved his hair for another role.

(679) Michelle Gomez was in line to play Ms. Delphox in Time Heist but couldn't make the audition. She was of course later cast as Missy.

(680) Matt Smith shot his cameo for Deep Breath during the production of The Time of the Doctor.

(681) In the episode Resolution, a Dalek is defeated by a microwave oven!

(682) The 'bootstrap paradox' is mentioned in Before the Flood. A bootstrap paradox is a time travel paradox where an object or piece of information is sent back in time and

becomes the inspiration or cause of itself. In other words, the origin of the object or information is impossible to determine because it exists in a continuous loop.

(683) Reece Shearsmith played Rasmussen in Sleep No More and Patrick Troughton in An Adventure in Space and Time - which was a drama about William Hartnell written by Mark Gatiss.

(684) The comedian and radio presenter Frank Skinner appears in Mummy on the Orient Express. Skinner is a big fan of Doctor Who.

(685) The BBC defended their decision to put John Simm as the Master in the series ten trailer by pointing out that The Sun had already ruined the surprise by leaking this.

(686) The shot of a 'Dreg' claw scraping against a wall is used so many times in Orphan 55 you genuinely wonder if they ran out of footage in the editing room.

(687) Tom Baker's portrayal of the Fourth Doctor is often considered the defining interpretation of the character.

(688) The character Jack Robertson in the Chibnall era is clearly based on Donald Trump.

(689) Sacha Dhawan was supposed to be in Demons of the Punjab but couldn't do it because he was too busy. This turned out well though because when Sacha was free again he was cast as the Master.

(690) Peter Capaldi improvised some of his dialogue when he makes his first appearance at the end of The Time of the Doctor.

(691) A lot of fans don't like the way that in the 2024 series the TARDIS, instead of just materialising out of nowhere, flies and skids to a halt like a regular plane or spaceship.

(692) Alan Cumming said he based his voice in The Witchfinders on Malcolm Rifkind. Malcom Rifkind is a former Conservative politician who was Defence Secretary and Foreign Secretary during his career.

(693) The dog like Karvanista (Craige Els) in the Flux is part of an alien race called the Lupari. It turns out that the Lupari are actually trying to rescue humans from Earth before a mysterious planet destroying entity called the Flux rolls in.

(694) 'Bad Wolf' was a recurring symbol in the first season by Russell T Davies. This was a masterful hook to keep us intrigued.

(695) The Legend of the Sea Devils, for a 'special', is conspicuously on the short side at 47 minutes and the editing is bizarre to say the least. It feels like there are whole scenes missing and one suspects that insufficient coverage was produced.

(696) The comedian John Bishop was likeable as the companion Dan in the Chibnall era and proved to be a fairly clever choice of replacement for Bradley Walsh.

(697) The actors playing The Beatles in The Devil's Chord seem a bit on the old side to be playing the Fab Four.

(698) Jenna Coleman originally planned to leave the show after Death in Heaven but she was persuaded to stay on.

(699) Peter Capaldi clearly does a Tom Baker impersonation a

few times during his run as the Doctor.

(700) The kiss between Vastra and Jenny in Deep Breath was actually deleted in some Asian countries because it was a same sex (and inter species!) kiss.

(701) Peter Capaldi wore his wedding ring when he played the Doctor because he refused to take it off.

(702) The Dalek in the Chris Chibnall episode Resolution was operated completely by remote control on the set.

(703) Peter Capaldi's rambling and slightly overlong speech before he regenerates into Jodie Whittaker was actually something Peter came up with himself.

(704) You can buy a number of Doctor Who themed board games and puzzles.

(705) There were some Doctor Who action transfers back in the day - including a very spiffy Dalek Attack one. Action Transfers, also known as rub-on transfers, were an art-based children's pastime.

(706) Sacha Dhawan was left off the advance cast list for the Spyfall episodes so as to not ruin the surprise of the Master being back. Not that anyone would have twigged he was playing the Master!

(707) The first Doctor Who story to be released on DVD was The Five Doctors. This was in 1999.

(708) Before playing the Master, Sacha Dhawan played Waris Hussein in An Adventure in Space and Time. Waris Hussein directed the first ever Doctor Who story.

(709) The Five-ish Doctors is a Doctor Who comedy special in which Peter Davison, Colin Baker, and Sylvester McCoy try to sneak their way into the 50th anniversary special.

(710) Robert Glenister played Thomas Edison in Nikola Tesla's Night of Terror. He was previously in The Caves of Androzani.

(711) Miriam Margolyes provided the voice of the Meep in The Star Beast.

(712) Colin Baker said when he played the Doctor he was unaware of the extent of the backstage chaos and feuding going on in relation to John Nathan Turner.

(713) John Nathan Turner said he had no interest in science fiction when he was growing up.

(714) Peter Davison expressed some disappointment when Jodie Whittaker was cast because he felt the Doctor was a rare example of a good male role model for boys.

(715) Peter Davison had to delete his social media for a bit after he said he didn't like the Doctor becoming a woman because he copped some flak.

(716) Colin Baker later said he regretted not filming his regeneration because in hindsight he had let the fans down by not doing that.

(717) Neil Patrick Harris is a magician and got to show off some of his magic skills in The Giggle.

(718) Colin Baker was furious when Eric Saward said in Starburst he was miscast as the Doctor because Eric had been his friend and often visited Colin's home. Colin would later

refuse to attend conventions if he knew that Eric Saward was going to be there.

(719) John Nathan Turner didn't like K-9 because he thought it was cheap for K-9 to get the Doctor out of trouble rather than the Doctor's ingenuity.

(720) Paul McGann shot his contribution to The Power of the Doctor alone and didn't get to meet Jodie Whittaker that day. He said he did meet Janet Fielding though.

(721) Russell T Davies, Mark Gatiss and Gareth Roberts all wrote Doctor Who stories for Virgin Publishing before the television show came back.

(722) The church used in The Church on Ruby Road was St Mary's Church near Newport

(723) John Nathan Turner said he never considered anyone but Colin Baker to play the Sixth Doctor.

(724) Selfridges sold a Dalek cake in their London shop during Christmas 1965.

(725) The Ninth Doctor and Rose Tyler are big fans of chips.

(726) You could actually buy Dalek wallpaper in the 1960s.

(727) The Fifteenth Doctor has a jukebox in his TARDIS.

(728) As part of the promotion for the show, Jon Pertwee appeared as the Doctor on boxes of Kellogs' Sugar Smacks cereal.

(729) The first Dalek toys came out in 1965.

(730) Kevin McNally, who played Professor Jericho in Village of the Angels, was in The Twin Dilemma as Hugo Lang.

(731) There is a theory that the BBC left John Nathan Turner in charge of Doctor Who for so long because that way he couldn't work on any of their other shows!

(732) Jon Pertwee was in 128 episodes as the Doctor.

(733) Doctor Who has been referenced in The Simpsons and Futurama.

(734) At the end of Revolution of the Daleks, Jack says he is off to catch up with Gwen from Torchwood.

(735) A production company headed by Peter Litton, George Dugdale and John Humphreys secured the film rights for Doctor Who from the BBC in the late 1980s. The script they produced was called Doctor Who: Last of the Time Lords and had the Doctor hopping around the galaxy trying to stop an all powerful entity from being created. Alan Rickman, Rutger Hauer and Donald Sutherland were alleged to be in contention to play the Doctor. When the film failed to go into production by 1994 the rights reverted back to the BBC.

Peter Litton, George Dugdale and John Humphreys, who had secured backing from a European studio to make the film, were furious and took legal action.

(736) The studio that Peter Litton, George Dugdale and John Humphreys got backing from was Lumière. By all accounts Lumière wanted to do their own script. They also wanted Pierce Brosnan to play the Doctor. This was only a year or two before Brosnan was cast as James Bond.

(737) The episode Full Circle takes some inspiration from Creature from the Black Lagoon. Creature from the Black Lagoon was released in 1954 and directed by Jack Arnold from a screenplay by Harry Essex. In the lush and somewhat foreboding environment of the Amazonian rain forest Dr Carl Maia (Antonio Moreno) makes a most extraordinary discovery. A fossilized hand with fins and claws no less. He decides to put a team together to travel down river to the mythic Black Lagoon in search of more evidence of this uncanny nature. Saddling up are Dr David Reed (Richard Carlson), Reed's girlfriend Kay Lawrence (Julie Adams), Dr Mark Williams (Richard Denning), and Dr Edwin Thompson (Whit Bissel). But Lucas (Nestor Paiva) - the Captain of their chartered boat "Rita" - tells them about the spooky legend of the man-fish that that resides at the Black Lagoon. A humanoid creature with gills and scales. Like a cross between a lizard, a fish and a synchronized swimmer.

They all soon realise that this apparently ludicrous tale is all too true and eventually make unpleasant contact with "The Gill-Man" (played by Ben Chapman on land and Ricou Browning underwater), resulting in more than a few deaths.

(738) David Tennant said he had no input into how he played the Doctor. He just played what he was given. Peter Capaldi said the same thing.

(739) The Doctor and the Master knew each other as children. Their history is long and knotty to say the least.

(740) UNIT was introduced in 1968's The Invasion.

(741) The highest rated NuWho Christmas specials on IMDB are A Christmas Carol and The Husbands of River Song - which both have a rating of 8.5 out of 10.

(742) The Ghost Monument was shot on location in South Africa.

(743) The Master has a Tissue Compression Eliminator which can be used to shrink people.

(744) Chris Barrie is alleged to have been a candidate to play the Doctor when the show came back after its long hiatus. It would have been strange to have the Doctor look like Arnold Rimmer!

(745) Tom Baker said that Philip Hinchcliffe was the best producer he worked with on the show during his run as the Doctor.

(746) William Hartnell said he didn't like the detour into horror the show took in the 1970s after he left because he felt Doctor Who should primarily be for children.

(747) Steven Moffat pictured Kate Winslet when he devised the character River Song. The chances of Kate Winslet actually playing the part were remote though because she was a pretty big film star.

(748) Mark Gatiss, who wrote An Adventure in Space and Time, said he would love to write a follow up drama about Doctor Who in the 1980s and how it was put on ice in 1985 and then cancelled.

(749) Stephen Fry was hired to write an episode of Doctor Who when the show came back in 2005 but it was never made because he didn't have time to complete it. Fry's story apparently took place in the 1920s.

(750) Sarah Jane Smith was an undercover journalist when she

first met the Doctor.

(751) It is sometimes reported that Nicola Bryant tested to Captain Janeway in Star Trek: Voyager. Nicola said this wasn't true though.

(752) There was definitely something of Harpo Marx in Tom Baker's version of the Doctor.

(753) We learn in The Ghost Monument that Ryan Sinclair is a fan of the Call of Duty video games.

(754) Steven Moffat said the reason he didn't cast a female Doctor when he was showrunner was because he wanted to cast Matt Smith and then Peter Capaldi.

(755) Chris Chibnall said that he never looked at any online Doctor Who discussions or comments about the show when he was the showrunner.

(756) In the episode 73 Yards, it is never explained what the older Ruby says to people to scare them away.

(757) The Doctor's TARDIS contains a library and a swimming pool.

(758) The TARDIS in the Peter Cushing films was the one that looked the most like a real police box. Steven Moffat actually asked for Matt Smith's TARDIS to look like the Peter Cushing one when he took over as showrunner.

(759) When the Doctor first stole his TARDIS it looked like a silver cylinder.

(760) Physicists have proposed different methods for potential

time travel, such as wormholes, black holes, and cosmic strings.

(761) One of the criticisms of the second era of Russell T Davies is that he seems to be recycling stuff from his first era. There don't seem to be many new ideas.

(762) Steven Moffat said he didn't put the Eighth Doctor in The Day of the Doctor because he felt the 'War Doctor' theme didn't suit that Doctor.

(763) Retrospectives of 1980s Doctor Who tend to give one the impression that none of the bosses at the BBC liked John Nathan Turner very much.

(764) Prior to the 2023 anniversary specials, rumours circulated that Sigourney Weaver had been on the set and was due to appear in them. This rumour turned out to be fake.

(765) In her first episode, The Thirteenth Doctor, separated from the TARDIS, constructs her own sonic from spare parts, steel, and spoons.

(766) The shooting location for the farewell between the Doctor and Rose in Doomsday was Southerndown Beach near Bridgend.

(767) Doctor Who was introduced to American television in 1982 and became quite cultish.

(768) Paul McGann said he once met Tom Baker in a recording studio and Tom had no idea who he was!

(769) There were references to Doctor Who in the sitcom The Big Bang Theory.

(770) You can buy TARDIS themed mugs, blankets, and pillows.

(771) The original TARDIS console was green so that it would be visible in black and white.

(772) The lighting in the Thirteenth Doctor's TARDIS can turn blue. We see it turn blue after she witnesses that Gallifrey has been destroyed.

(773) John Nathan Turner once said you can't win when you are the boss of Doctor Who. Whatever you do a portion of the fanbase will moan!

(774) The Chris Chibnall era of Doctor Who had a fantastic spooky title sequence.

(775) Jon Pertwee said he wasn't a big fan of the Daleks. He thought they were a bit silly.

(776) The Doctor is a moral compass, advocating for peace, justice, and empathy in the face of conflict.

(777) The location used for when the TARDIS lands in Wales at the start of 73 Yards was Giltar Point in Tenby.

(778) Vastra is a Silurian warrior living in Victorian London. She is a very good detective.

(779) Peter Davison said that when he played the Doctor he always prided himself on knowing the script inside out because he thought it was important for him to fully understand the story in order to play it correctly.

(780) One of the problems with the Thirteenth Doctor's

TARDIS interior is that it feels a lot like a television studio. While the 'crystal cave' theme was interesting the design didn't quite work in the end.

(781) John Nathan Turner started out as an aspiring actor but moved into production when he realised he wasn't good enough to be a professional actor.

(782) Russell T Davies said that with the 2024 series he leaned the show more into fantasy (as opposed to undiluted science fiction).

(783) Going into The Power of the Doctor there was a degree of fan scepticism due to the fact that this was not only Jodie's final episode but would also feature the return of the Master and the companions Tegan and Ace. How could Chris Chibnall possibly wrap up the Jodi era in a satisfactory way and produce a coherent and decent episode in what sounded like an overstuffed final special? Given Chibnall's track record when it came to finales one can understand why some feared the worst. Expectations were also unavoidably lowered by the abysmal penultimate special Legend of the Sea Devils.

Going into this final special you probably would have got long odds that Chris Chibnall could pull this off and go out on a high note. Amazingly though, Chris Chibnall proved the doubters wrong because The Power of the Doctor is actually a lot of fun and one of the very best episodes of his era.

(784) There have been Doctor Who themed Advent calendars.

(785) There have been some Doctor Who references in the Fallout video game series.

(786) Alex Kingston is 20 years older than Matt Smith. She said

she felt quite 'motherly' towards him playing their romantic scenes in Doctor Who!

(787) In the cultish late 80s film Bill and Ted's Excellent Adventure, a telephone booth is used as a time travel machine. The makers of this film claim they were unaware of Doctor Who and the TARDIS when they had this idea. It seems a bit fanciful to believe that not a single Hollywood creative involved in the film had heard of Doctor Who or the TARDIS!

(788) The first Doctor Who magazine was published in 1979.

(789) The football stadium in 73 Yards is the Cardiff City Stadium.

(790) Russell T Davies said The Giggle was originally going to have Wilfred Mott passing away (Bernard Cribbins had sadly died in real life after shooting one scene) but he was persuaded to leave Wilf alive in the Doctor Who universe.

(791) When the show came back in 2005, the TARDIS interior was designed to look a bit battered and dirty to indicate that the Doctor had been through a lot since we last saw him.

(792) The plot of Legend of the Sea Devils has Madam Ching (Crystal Yu) raiding a village and releasing the Sea Devil Marsissus from a stone statue. Madame Ching was a prominent pirate during the early 19th century in the South China Sea.

(793) The lamp for the original TARDIS in Classic Who was replaced in series two.

(794) In the episode The Devil's Chord we see the Doctor and Ruby walk across the zebra crossing at Abbey Road. This scene

was actually filmed in Cardiff. They just found a Cardiff street to double for Abbey Road.

(795) Tom Baker was 40 years-old when he was cast as the Doctor.

(796) The Doctor Who ratings wobbled in 1980 because ITV were showing the American series Buck Rogers in the 25th Century on the other side.

(797) The Doctor's car Bessie first appeared in Doctor Who and the Silurians.

(798) Nardole is a humanoid cyborg who was reassembled by the Doctor.

(799) The First Doctor smoked a pipe in An Unearthly Child.

(800) The first Doctor Who action figures were released in 1977.

(801) Time travel fiction like Doctor Who frequently delves into paradoxes.

(802) There are a smattering of episodes where the Doctor displays telepathic abilities.

(803) UNIT stands for the United Nations Intelligence Taskforce.

(804) Paul Stone, who produced The Box of Delights, Tom's Midnight Garden and The Lion, the Witch, and the Wardrobe for television in the 1980s, was offered the chance to replace John Nathan Turner as the boss of Doctor Who in 1986 but he wasn't interested in the position.

(805) No one apart from David Tennant was considered for the Tenth Doctor. Luckily for the production team he agreed to do it.

(806) Colin Baker's Doctor always wore a cat badge on his costume.

(807) Mandip Gill said she wasn't a fan of Doctor Who before she was cast as Yaz so she had to watch some of the show to get up to speed.

(808) The American singer and actor Jonathan Groff, the guest star in the 2024 story Rogue, had never seen Doctor Who before when he was cast in this episode.

(809) The planet Gallifrey is in the constellation of Kasterborous.

(810) According to the theory of relativity, time travel is theoretically possible, but only forward in time.

(811) A section of Doctor Who fans seem to love arguing about viewing figures and whether they are good, bad, or merely average. The changing landscape of how we consume entertainment makes analysing viewing figures more difficult than it used to be but the figures for the 2024 series plainly seemed to indicate that the show's viewer base is declining.

(812) The Doctor was asexual in Classic Who but this hasn't always been the case in NuWho.

(813) The planet Gallifrey is 250 million light years away.

(814) Russell T Davies said that when you write a Doctor Who script you have to shut the Doctor up in the story sometimes

because otherwise the Doctor will just explain the plot and solve everything too easily.

(815) The Star Beast was adapted from a comic by Dave Gibbons and Pat Mills which came out in 1980. Dave Gibbons and Pat Mills visited the set of the 2023 television adaptation.

(816) Throughout its long history, Doctor Who has tackled complex ethical questions and moral dilemmas.

(817) David Tennant said he probably would have become a teacher if acting hadn't worked out for him.

(818) One of the Doctor's nicknames is The Oncoming Storm.

(819) Sylvester McCoy only has eleven lines of dialogue in the Doctor Who television movie.

(820) Amy Pond's middle name is Jessica.

(821) William Russell, who played Ian Chesterton, said he was very impressed by the way William Hartnell consistently adhered to specific buttons when he was operating that TARDIS console because this made it more realistic.

(822) The science fiction writer Nigel Kneale (of Quatermass fame) was asked to write for Doctor Who in its early days but declined the offer. Kneale didn't like Doctor Who and never had anything nice to say about it.

(823) Due to a mix up with the moulds, the first Doctor Who action figure looked more like Gareth Hunt than Tom Baker!

(824) Big Finish released their first Doctor Who audio adventure in 1999.

(825) Fans often cosplay as their favorite Doctor Who characters at conventions and events.

(826) Bonnie Langford said the moment where Mel finds the Sixth Doctor's costume in Empire of Death was quite emotional for her because it brought back a lot of memories.

(827) John Nathan Turner would do interviews at fan events when he was the producer and subject himself to questions and a few grillings. You probably couldn't imagine Russell T Davies putting himself in a situation where he had to listen to fan complaints about the show.

(828) The TARDIS is bigger on the inside thanks to dimensional engineering.

(829) The Tenth Doctor has a dislike of pears.

(830) Peter Davision later said he felt John Nathan Turner wasn't qualified to be in charge of Doctor Who because he was a producer and not a writer. When the show came back in 2005 the new structure was that the lead producer (showrunner) was also the main writer.

(831) Julia Sawalha tested for the part of Ace. This was not long before she got her big break in Steven Moffat's cultish children's show Press Gang.

(832) Peter Davison, Colin Baker and Sylvester McCoy all disliked the question mark motif that John Nathan Turner put on their costumes.

(833) K-9 being axed from Doctor Who by John Nathan Turner made headlines in Britain and there was even a petition to bring him back. This was what prompted the K-9 special. John

Nathan turner was basically ordered by the BBC to do something with K-9.

(834) Sylvester McCoy's Doctor was known for his umbrella.

(835) In series ten, the Doctor has a mysterious vault in which he is clearly keeping someone contained. It turned out to be Missy but there were a lot of fan theories that he had the First Doctor down there. The First Doctor, played by David Bradley, did eventually turn up though as Capaldi's run drew to a close.

(836) The Third Doctor spending so much time on Earth was not just to reduce costs but also because the producers felt it would make the show more relatable.

(837) Brian Cox plays Sydney Newman (the head of BBC drama when Doctor Who was created) in An Adventure in Space and Time. Brian Cox said that when he was a very young actor he actually met Sydney Newman in real life.

(838) Sylvester McCoy said he often couldn't make much sense of the scripts when he was on Doctor Who.

(839) The Doctor's longest-serving companion is Sarah Jane Smith.

(840) When the show came back in 2005, Russell T Davies had a strict policy of not hiring any writers from the Classic Who days. He wanted a complete fresh slate.

(841) The book the Doctor reads in the 1996 television movie is The Time Machine.

(842) The Daleks' catchphrase is "Exterminate!"

(843) Colin Baker apparently didn't have to audition when he was chosen to be the Doctor.

(844) The 1996 Doctor Who television movie brought back the sonic screwdriver. It hadn't been used in the television show since 1982.

(845) William Hartnell's Doctor was a bit spikier than those that immediately followed.

(846) Steven Moffat said he was open to casting a mature actor as the Eleventh Doctor but Matt Smith was simply the best person for the job.

(847) Colin Baker said he thought that Tom Baker's cameo in The Day of the Doctor was a bit pointless.

(848) The Five(ish) Doctors Reboot depicts Peter Davision as a washed up actor desperate for work. In reality though Peter arguably had the best post-Doctor career of anyone from Classic Who.

(849) During the Colin Baker run on Doctor Who, the production team were rather confused by conflicting instructions from the BBC. The big boss Michael Grade wanted more humour while the head of drama Jonathan Powell complained the scripts were too comedic!

(850) As many people pointed out, the episode Dot and Bubble feels very inspired by Black Mirror.

(851) References to Doctor Who were awash in Queer as Folk - which was the show that put Russell T Davies on the map and made him an important figure in British television.

(852) Before the 2024 series had even come out there was much media chatter about how Millie Gibson had been fired. This media chatter was wide of the mark because Ruby Sunday's story arc was completed in the 2024 series and it was announced Millie Gibson would appear in some episodes in the following season.

(853) The 1996 Doctor Who television movie has a very cosy TARDIS interior with a steampunk feel and comfy chair.

(854) Iain Cuthbertson, who guest starred opposite Tom Baker in the 1978 story The Ribos Operation, was considered for the Fifth Doctor.

(855) The Thirteenth Doctor selected her costume in a charity shop.

(856) When he left the show after The Power of the Doctor, Chris Chibnall asked Russell T Davies not to tell him anything about the forthcoming anniversary specials so that he could just watch them as a fan without knowing what was going to happen.

(857) David Tennant said he wouldn't mind appearing in Star Trek one day.

(858) There has been Doctor Who LEGO.

(859) The Doctor has a strong sense of justice and often stands up for the underdog.

(860) Sylvester McCoy wore his own hat as the Doctor.

(861) At one point the 1996 Doctor Who movie was to be a complete American reboot of the television series. Thankfully

this didn't happen in the end.

(862) The Torchwood Institute was created by Queen Victoria.

(863) Eve Myles played Gwen in Torchwood but was previously a maid in The Unquiet Dead.

(864) The Ninth Doctor and Eleventh Doctor never encountered the Master in the show.

(865) The house used for the stately home in the 2024 episode Rogue was Tredegar House in Newport.

(866) As many pointed out, one of the main problems with the Sixth Doctor's costume is that it made him look like a court jester.

(867) Patrick Troughton had a famous death as Father Brennan in the 1976 horror film The Omen.

(868) The first episode of Doctor Who aired the day after President John F. Kennedy was assassinated, leading to low viewership for the premiere.

(869) Jean Marsh has a cameo in An Adventure in Space and Time. Jean Marsh appeared in the Hartnell era and was also once married to Jon Pertwee.

(870) After the death of Elisabeth Sladen, Steven Moffat decided not to have Sarah Jane's death mentioned when he took over as showrunner. Her fate was left open ended. However, in the 2023 episode The Giggle the Fifteenth and Fourteenth Doctors do seem to acknowledge that Sarah Jane has passed away.

(871) One of the most moving moments in An Adventure in Space and Time comes when William Hartnell is filming his last scene as the Doctor and looks up to see Matt Smith's Doctor beside him. For a recent repeat of An Adventure in Space and Time the BBC replaced Matt Smith with Ncuti Gatwa. Presumably, An Adventure in Space and Time will just feature whoever the current Doctor is in this scene each time it is repeated.

(872) There was a Who/Star Trek comic book crossover with Star Trek: The Next Generation/Doctor Who: Assimilation². in the story the Eleventh Doctor teams up with Captain Picard to battle an alliance between the Borg and the Cybermen.

(873) Barry Letts had intended to cast an older William Hartnell type actor as the Fourth Doctor but he changed his mind when Tom Baker came onto his radar.

(874) The Whomobile was a hovercraft type vehicle that could also fly. Jon Pertwee helped design this vehicle.

(875) Classic Who often used to show us other rooms in the TARDIS and companions had their own bedrooms. They haven't done this so much in NuWho but it did happen now and again. Nu Who episodes like Journey to the Centre of the TARDIS did show us more of the ship.

(876) It seems plausible to suggest that the Cybermen were at least some sort of influence on the Borg in Star Trek.

(877) Tom Baker described shooting his cameo in The Day of the Doctor as 'bloody boring' because of the waiting around but said he did enjoy acting with Matt Smith.

(878) Ncuti Gatwa was homeless for a period before he was

famous and spent three months sleeping on sofas belonging to friends.

(879) The Curse of Fatal Death is a comedic Doctor Who special written by Steven Moffat and aired in 1999 for Red Nose Day. The story follows the Doctor as he faces off against his old enemy, the Master, in a battle that spans over four different regenerations. Throughout the special, the Doctor is repeatedly killed and regenerated, each time taking on a new form and personality. However, it soon becomes clear that each regeneration is cursed, as the Doctor's com companions keep getting killed in various comical ways. The cast in this special included Rowan Atkinson and Joanna Lumley.

(880) The Doctor's companion, K-9, was originally created as a one-off character, but due to his popularity, he became a recurring companion.

(881) The 2024 series of Doctor Who was shot back to back with the series that followed. Some fans felt this was a risky move because it meant that the producers would be unable to take feedback into account and make any course corrections.

(882) The companion Yaz was one of the biggest failures of the Chris Chibnall era for some fans in that she was there from start to finish but just ended up as this weird blank of a character who we completely forgot about the moment the Chibnall era ended. Maybe it might be nice if one day Yaz made another appearance in the show with a different writer and Doctor. It would certainly be interesting to see Mandip Gill have another crack at the part in different circumstances.

(883) Richard Hearne was interviewed for the part of the Fourth Doctor. Hearne was an actor and comedian best known for his comic character Mr Pastry.

(884) The Flux is a very Star Trek type plot device.

(885) Arc of Infinity did some shooting in Amsterdam.

(886) Peter Davison, Colin Baker and Sylvester McCoy all said that Patrick Troughton was their favourite Doctor.

(887) Charlie Higson's 'office joker' character Colin Hunt in The Fast Show was partly inspired by Colin Baker's Doctor. Like the Sixth Doctor, Colin Hunt has a shock of curly hair and a garish dress sense.

(888) Peri's full name is Perpugilliam Brown.

(889) The 'alternative' comedian Alexei Sayle played DJ in Revelation of the Daleks. It is sometimes reported that Alexei Sayle was considered for the part of the Doctor after Colin Baker was axed. It may have just been a joke on Sayle's part.

(890) Peter Davision said he was a bit envious of Doctor Who when it came back in 2005 because he felt the writing and production values were better than when he was on the show in the 1980s.

(891) The Master's flying Australian bush house TARDIS at the end of Spyfall is a nice riff on The Wizard of Oz.

(892) Twenty episodes of NuWho have scored 9 or over (out of ten obviously) on IMDB. However, not a single episode since the Capaldi era has managed this feat - which does tend to indicate that the Chibnall and second RTD eras haven't quite landed with audiences in the way older NuWho did.

(893) The new TARDIS interior introduced in The Star Beast is certainly the largest and most spectacular interior we've seen.

However, critics of this interior feel it seems very empty and sterile.

(894) In season ten, UNIT now operated from a rural base in the countryside close to London.

(896) Russell T Davies said he considered having Peter Purves make an appearance in The Giggle but this obviously never happened in the end.

(897) Paradise Towers patently takes some inspiration from J.G. Ballard's novel High-Rise.

(898) Walls had some Doctor Who themed ice lollies in the 1960s. You got a Doctor Who action card with your lolly.

(899) In the Who universe Vastra and Jenny were the inspiration for Holmes & Watson.

(900) The breakfast cereal Weetabix did a couple of Doctor who themed promotions in the 1970s.

(901) It would have cost you nearly £40 to buy Revenge of the Cybermen on home video when the BBC first released it. £40 was quite a lot of money in 1983.

(902) Colin Baker said he was disappointed that John Nathan Turner didn't make a stand when Michael Grade asked for him to be fired as the Doctor.

(903) It was the introduction of the Daleks which made Doctor Who a big sensation. The BBC hadn't predicted this though. In fact, the producer Donald Wilson thought that Terry Nation's first Dalek script was so awful it shouldn't be made.

(904) William Hartnell was in quite poor health near the end of his run as the Doctor and had trouble remembering his lines.

(905) The Doctor Who episode Hide reminded many of the premise of the film The Legend of Hell House. The Legend of Hell House is a 1973 British horror film directed by John Hough and adapted by Richard Matheson from his own novel. The film is much in the vein of The Haunting and House on Haunted Hill and revolves around an investigation into a spooky, fog-shrouded country mansion.

(906) Peter Davison said they wrote to Tom Baker three times inviting him to take part in The Five(ish) Doctors Reboot but Tom never bothered to respond.

(907) Edgar Wright said that his film The World's End was inspired by the Doctor Who episode The Android Invasion.

(908) Nigel Kneale (of Quatermass fame) often complained that Doctor Who (in his view) ripped off some of his own stories.

(909) The Tenth Doctor undermines the Prime Minister Harriet Jones by suggesting to one of her aides that she looks tired. This is apparently something one of Margaret Thatcher's aides said about her shortly before she was removed as prime minister by her own party.

(910) The first time we met UNIT in Classic Who they operated from a Hercules military transport plane.

(911) Funko Pop! have done a range of Doctor Who figures.

(912) Peter Brachacki was the BBC designer who created the

original TARDIS set.

(913) The two highest peaks for average (British) Doctor Who viewing figures are Tom Baker in the 1970s and David Tennant circa 2009. The 2024 series with the Fifteenth Doctor has the lowest average number of viewers.

(914) The highest rated episode from the Chris Chibnall era on IMDB is Village of the Angels - which has a rating of 7.7 out of 10.

(915) John Nathan Turner said he bumped off Adric because the TARDIS was getting too crowded.

(916) Jon Pertwee said he disliked some of the 'scientific claptrap' he had to dispense as the Doctor because it was a pain to remember.

(917) The character Leela was inspired by Loana in One Million Years B.C. One Million Years B.C. is a 1966 film by the legendary Hammer Studios directed by Don Chaffey. The film is a daft but colourful and ambitious romp depicting the struggles of early cavemen types as they battle each other and various assorted dinosaurs and gigantic creatures which co-exist alongside humans here in ahistorical Flintstones fashion.

"This is a story of long, long ago, when the world was just beginning," informs a narrator at the start of the film over rolling clouds and lava flows. Tumak (John Richardson) is a hunter with the violent Rock tribe but after a ruck with his chieftain father Akhoba (Robert Brown) he is exiled and wanders the sun-drenched lunar-like landscapes dodging anachronistic dinosaurs until he encounters a more peaceful and advanced group known as the Shell tribe living by the sea. Tumak becomes an accepted member of the tribe when he saves a little girl from an Allosaurus and also takes an understandable shine to Loana (Raquel Welch), a supermodel cavegirl with a fur-skin bikini and fake eyelashes. When he is cast out from the Shell tribe for trying to pilfer somebody's spear, Tumak takes Loana on a long trek back to his old tribe in an attempt to secure his birthright.

(918) Planet of Fire used the Canary Islands as a shooting location.

(919) Jon Pertwee was already famous (especially through his radio work) in Britain when he became the Doctor but that wasn't the case with Tom Baker. Tom wasn't very famous at all when he landed the part of the Doctor.

(920) An Unearthly Child suggests that Susan named the TARDIS. Later on though it was implied that TARDIS was a common term used by Time Lords.

(921) Sheffield featured a lot in the Chibnall era because he wanted to get away from the show going to London all the time.

(922) In a 1990s interview, John Nathan Turner said he felt that Tom Baker was given too much freedom and not enough direction in his portrayal of the Doctor.

(923) An Adventure in Space and Time missed out on a Hugo award because it was beaten by the Game of Thrones episode The Rains of Castamere. This was somewhat ironic as David Bradley played William Hartnell in An Adventure in Space and Time and the evil Walder Frey in The Rains of Castamere.

(924) David Bradley was in his seventies when he played William Hartnell in An Adventure in Space and Time. This

made him considerably older than Hartnell had been when he played the Doctor.

(925) Peter Davison said that one of the reasons he left Doctor Who is that he didn't think the scripts were very good.

(926) David Bradley also appeared in The Sarah Jane Adventures.

(927) Tom Baker said he had agreed to appear in The Sarah Jane Adventures but sadly the death of Elisabeth Sladen meant this never happened.

(928) William Russell, who played Ian Chesterton, said that when he first went to a fan convention he could barely answer any questions because he couldn't actually remember that much about Doctor Who!

(929) Carole Ann Ford said that when they made the early Doctor Who episodes the air conditioning at the BBC wasn't very good so the cast would sometimes get quite sweaty and hot.

(930) Peter Cushing said that when he made the Amicus Dr Who films he wasn't that familiar with the television show because he didn't watch television.

(931) The Ood were inspired by the works of H.P. Lovecraft.

(932) Time travel has long been a staple in fiction, both on the page and the screen. In 1895 the HG Wells novella The Time Machine, a classic tale of fantasy, was published and inspired myriad time travel stories.

(933) John Hurt was 73 when he was cast as the War Doctor.

(934) The Eleventh and Twelfth Doctor never had any adventures with Captain Jack Harkness in the show.

(935) Newt Scamander in Fantastic Beasts was patently very inspired by the Doctor - especially the Eleventh Doctor.

(936) Vinette Robinson played Rosa Parks in Rosa but was previously Abi Lerner in the episode 42.

(937) The Pandorica is stored near Stonehenge.

(938) Christopher Lloyd was in contention to play the Master in the 1996 television movie but this obviously didn't transpire in the end.

(939) There is literally nowhere to sit down in the TARDIS used by the Fourteenth and Fifteenth Doctor!

(940) Eric Saward said his problem with Colin Baker's Doctor is he felt Colin was too 'hammy' and more of a character actor than leading man.

(941) David Tennant said he was a bit daunted at first by taking over as the Doctor because Christopher Eccleston had been so good in the role.

(942) There are Doctor Who Minecraft mods.

(943) Michelle Gomez said she was given a lot of freedom to tailor the part of Missy to her own style and direction.

(944) Catherine Tate said being in Doctor Who was the best job she's ever had.

(945) John Leeson (who supplied the voice) said that K-9 went

'haywire' on the set a few times.

(946) In the Chris Chibnall episode Resolution we are told that UNIT doesn't exist due to budget cuts.

(947) Since the show came back in 2005, only Russell T Davies, Steven Moffat, and Chris Chibnall have been in charge of it.

(948) Alan Rickman was one of the actors considered to play the Doctor in the 1996 Doctor Who movie.

(949) The Doctor and Ruby sing during the goblin musical number in The Church on Ruby Road. It would probably be fair to say that this sort of stuff isn't to the taste of all Who fans.

(950) Jon Pertwee said he loved Fridays on Doctor Who because that's when he got his cheque from the BBC!

(951) The Sontarans were created by Robert Holmes in 1972.

(952) The Time Vortex is a swirling mass of energy that exists outside of time and space in the Doctor Who universe. It is often described as a gateway between different points in time and can be used by Time Lords, like the Doctor, to travel through time and space. The Time Vortex is depicted as a swirling, colourful tunnel of energy in the TV show.

(953) The groaning noise the TARDIS makes is a consequence of the Doctor leaving the brakes on.

(954) It is sometimes suggested that the Doctor might have been Merlin in King Arthur's court.

(955) When the BBC tried to trademark the TARDIS in the

1990s the Metropolitan Police challenged this case because they had, afterall, invented the police box in the first place. Nonetheless, the BBC won the case.

(956) When it comes to NuWho, Christopher Eccleston's debut got the highest figures.

(957) 1979's City of Death got the highest viewing figures in Britain of any Doctor Who episode.

(958) David Tennant said that Tom Baker's Doctor inspired him to become an actor.

(959) Tom Baker did commercials for Prime Computers in the 1980s as the Doctor.

(960) At a 2024 convention appearance, Christopher Eccleston said he would only consider playing the Doctor on television again if Russell T Davies and his production team were fired.

(961) The TARDIS was designed to be operated by six people.

(962) While the episode Daleks in Manhattan does feature some genuine New York footage, David Tennant and Freema Agyeman never actually went to New York to shoot anything.

(963) Steven Moffat has implied that (in the Who universe) the term 'Doctor' for a medical healer/expert actually derives from the Doctor.

(964) The exterior shots in Dot and Bubble were shot at Swansea University Bay Campus.

(965) When he stood down as the Doctor, Peter Capaldi suggested that Frances de la Tour should replace him.

(966) The Thirteenth Doctor inspired the first ever Doctor Who Barbie Doll.

(967) Liam Cunningham tested to play the Eighth Doctor. Liam would later become best known for his role as Davos Seaworth in Game of Thrones.

(968) Jodie Whittaker said that the Thirteenth Doctor was closer to her own personality than other roles she had played in the past.

(969) A full size TARDIS prop built for Dr Who and The Daleks went up for sale at a recent auction. The starting price for bids was £8,000.

(970) A 60th anniversary poll for Doctor Who magazine voted Heaven Sent as the best episode.

(971) A poll by YouGov found that 94% of the British public had heard of Doctor Who. The remaining 6% have obviously been living in a cave with no access to television!

(972) The Fifteenth Doctor seems to cry at the drop of a hat. Not everyone was pleased about this.

(973) It is made fairly clear in the Chibnall era that Yaz has romantic feelings for the Doctor and that maybe the Doctor has feelings for Yaz but doesn't really know how to respond. With this in mind, some fans noted it was slightly strange that as soon as Thirteen regenerated into Fourteen the first thing Fourteen did was not visit Yaz but start knocking around with Donna Noble again!

(974) Jon Pertwee released a song in 1972 called Who Is The Doctor in which he delivered a monologue to music. The song

didn't chart and is quite obscure today.

(975) The Weeping Angels are known as the Lonely Assassins.

(976) The Victorian version of Clara was originally going to be the Eleventh Doctor's companion after Amy but Steven Moffat changed his mind and decided to have a modern version of Clara as the companion. It has been alleged that the BBC wanted a modern companion to make the show more relatable. Many fans though liked the Victorian Clara more.

(977) Christopher Eccleston, in what was seen as a surprising move, returned to the role of the Doctor again in 2020 for some Big Finish audio adventures.

(978) We never really found out why the TARDIS threw the Thirteenth Doctor out when she first appeared after Twelve's regeneration.

(979) David Tennant said he came back for the anniversary specials because it was one last chance to play the Doctor again before he got too old.

(980) A poll by YouGov in 2019 had David Tennant as the most popular Doctor. Tom Baker was only third - which may indicate that a lot of voters were too young to experience much of Classic Who.

(981) The former Doctor Who companion Peter Purves later became the presenter of the dog show Crufts.

(982) Peter Capaldi complained about Doctor Who being moved around in the schedules when he was in the show.

(983) The hospital sets in the Doctor Who television film were

also used in The X-Files.

(984) There was a lot of speculation that the Paternoster Gang of Vastra, Strax, and Jenny were hoping to get their own spin-off show but this obviously never happened in the end.

(985) Jon Pertwee was a candidate to play Willy Wonka in the cult 1971 film Willy Wonka & the Chocolate Factory but he declined to pursue the part due to other commitments.

(986) In the episode World Enough and Time, Missy suggests the Doctor's real name is Doctor Who. Many saw this as Steven Moffat trolling the audience in a piece of mischief.

(987) The Sontarans come from a planet with high gravity - which explains their bulky short build.

(988) Golden Wonder did a six pack of crisps in 1986 with Colin Baker on the cover and a Doctor Who magazine inside.

(989) It was the director Rachel Talalay who had the idea of the Doctor running around the new TARDIS interior at the end of The Star Beast.

(990) Bonnie Langford's character Mel is from Pease Pottage. Pease Pottage is a village in the Mid Sussex District of West Sussex.

(991) The Golden Cross bar in Cardiff was used for the scene in The Church on Ruby Road where Ruby plays with her band.

(992) Believe it or not, in the early 1980s you could buy Doctor Who underpants from BHS.

(993) The Eleventh Doctor's TARDIS interior was the first to

feature different levels.

(994) The Android Invasion has some obvious similarities to The Earth Dies Screaming. The Earth Dies Screaming is a 1964 British science-fiction and horror film directed by Terence Fisher.

(995) Before he played the Doctor, Matt Smith was one of the final candidates to play the character Will in the cult comedy show The Inbetweeners. In the end it was Simon Bird who played this part.

(996) Rose Tyler and Captain Jack Harkness were named after the two main characters in the James Cameron film Titanic.

(997) Trial of a Timelord is what you might describe as 'on the nose' given that the show itself was essentially on trial at the time!

(998) Catherine Tate said she never really watched Doctor Who before she was in it but she did remember Tom Baker being famous as the Doctor when she was growing up.

(999) When it began, Doctor Who was shot at Lime Grove Studios in Shepherd's Bush. Lime Grove was one of the studios owned by the BBC. It was demolished in 1993.

(1000) William Russell said the food at Lime Grove Studios was so bad that the Doctor Who cast would bring a packed lunch so they could avoid the canteen!

Photo Credit

https://unsplash.com/photos/pink-blue-and-green-light-kD7bsGPsV4w

Dustin Humes

July 23, 2020